SCRIPTURE OF THE BLIND

YANNIS RITSOS

Translated from the Greek,
With an Introduction, by

KIMON FRIAR
and KOSTAS MYRSIADES

Scripture of the Blind

OHIO STATE UNIVERSITY PRESS: COLUMBUS

Library of Congress Cataloguing in Publication Data

Ritsos, Giannes, 1909–
  Scripture of the blind.

  English and Greek.
  I. Title.
PZ5629.I7S3   889'.1'32   78-14319
ISBN 0-8142-0298-5

ε

CONTENTS

Acknowledgments

A number of the poems in this collection have previously been published in the following periodicals: the *American Poetry Review* ("Naked Face," "Public Speech," "Monologue with Someone Hidden," "Uncertain Obligations," "Real Hands," "The Other Man," "Common Miracles," "The Dissonant Chord," "Imitation of an Imitation," "Face to Face," "Iconographers," "Patient Knowledge," "Indications," "Autumnal Correspondence," "Portioning Out," and "The Eyes of the Statues"); *Antaeus* ("Mute," "In the Same Quarter," "Nightly Performances," "Outline of a Nightmare," "The District 'Thimarakis,'" "After a Settlement of Debts," "Augmentation of the Unknown," "Fourth Nocturne," and "The Statue in the Cafe"); the *Antioch Review* ("Surveillance"); *Chelsea* ("The Earth's Attraction," "Secret Audience," and "Lightless"); the *Denver Quarterly* ("On the Television Screen" and "Opposition"); *Epoch* ("Hyalography of the Bath" and "The Earthen Adolescent"); *The Falcon* ("Meaningless Exception," "Modest Contrivances," "Demolished Shelters," "At the Harbor's Edge," "Relapse," "Vulnerability," "A Weary Thanksgiving," "Timidity," "Eyewitness," "Night Arrests," "Vespers," "Habitual Surprise," "Elsewhere," "Hues of a Cloud," "Solitary Discourse," "Silent Praise," "The Same Shout," "32 Years," "Ineffectual Oaths," "Caught in the Act," "Perpetual," "Blood Letting," "Vague Design," "The Dark Shop," "No Longer," "Constant Debt," "Evening Bar," "Change of Pace," and "Continuity"); *Grove Magazine* ("Without a Mirror Now," "Unfulfilled Promise," "St. Nicholas Station," "Spasmodically," "The Third Poem," "Transposition," "Doubtful Therapy," "Unburied," "The Meaning of Art," "Resistance to the Indefinite," "Anonymous Street," "Reticence," "Extinction," "Gradually Stripped Bare," "Midnight Cry," "Liter," "Symbolical," and "Hesitation"); the *Literary Review* ("Liturgical," "Simultaneously," "Way of Life," "Small Sonata," and "Stages of Ignorance"); *Mundus Artium* ("Justice"); the *Ohio Journal* ("Midnight Stroll," "Layers," "Like a Prayer," "The Electric Current Cut Off," "The Get-Away," "Questioning Conclusion," and "Twelve Hour Period"); and *Poet Lore* ("On Heroes," "General Malady," "Secret Exit," "That Which Is Heard Always," "The Same Theme," and "Under the Cloud").

I

In the general total of Yánnis Rítsos's multiple works, the poems
of average length are few. To fulfill the dual aspects of his charac-
ter, he seems to need, on the one hand, the long discursive poem
in which he may ramble almost to loquacious lengths, to rumi-
nate, to simplify, to merge past and present, to digress, to indulge
in mood and musical movement. But, on the other hand, he needs
equally the condensed, almost epigrammatical poem that is
sharp, cryptic, concrete, symbolistic, almost surrealistic in its
juxtaposition of seemingly unrelated objects or events. Extremes
meet, emotions stretched to tension suddenly turn into their op-
posites: love turns into hate, patriotism into treason, virtue into
sin. Such metamorphosis in a poet is the mark of an essentially
dramatic character.

Rítsos himself has written about his urge, since early childhood
in Laconia, to write laconic poems, recognizing that this is for
him no simple play on words but a temperamental necessity. This
need began to take on concrete form in 1938-41 with a series of
short poems entitled *Notes on the Margins of Time,* continued
later in 1946-47 with a group entitled *Parentheses,* and then in
1950-60 with a long series entitled *Exercises,* until they were crys-
tallized into their final form and given the general title of *Tes-
timonies A* (1963), *Testimonies B* (1966), and *Testimonies C*
(1966-67).

Poems that have followed in this mode have been given their
own individual titles, such as the ones in this book, *Scripture of
the Blind,* the explosive aftermath of Rítsos's bitter experience
when he was arrested immediately after the colonels' military
coup of 23 April 1967, sent to detention camps on various islands
in the Aegean, and exiled in Sámos. Finally, because he had
become seriously ill, and because of the great outcries throughout
Europe against his maltreatment, he was permitted to remain in

Athens, but under close surveillance. All these poems but one were written compulsively at white heat, sometimes two or three a day, in a concentrated two-month period between 28 September and 28 November, at the height of the junta years, when it seemed that tyranny, oppression, torture, and degradation were to be the fate of Greece for many more years to come. The poet's nightmare landscape in these poems is pervaded by grotesque images and absurdities dislocated and malformed by inhuman times: diplomats in top hats gathering eggs from a brilliantly lit chicken coop, old women picking out shoes to fit their hands, someone cutting off the five fingers of his hand in order to "believe in the indivisible," a naked baby abandoned in a large army boot, the poet holding the severed head of a doll, a dead crow placed as a head on a dead woman's wedding gown.

But there are other, more immediate images of the dictator's presence: firing squads, handcuffs, night arrests, betrayals, oppression, guards, gallows, death, exile, surgeons, rubber hose, identity cards, desertions, revolts, confessions behind which confessions are hidden, and the bitterness and emptiness of a menaced land. Oppression is also revealed in details of domestic life: the pall that hangs over the simplest family gathering, unmatched shoes, the red eggs of Easter and resurrection beside bread riddled with bullets, a vacuum cleaner run to cover the sound of shots, knives wrapped in bandages. At this domestic level, pain is neither avoidable nor resistable. It is so pervasive that it can no longer be considered abnormal. Rather, oppression becomes its own norm, that which has now become normal to the human species. Early in his surgical regime, Colonel Papadhópoulos notoriously likened Greece to the body of a sick woman who has been operated on and encased in plaster from her feet to her head. "And we shall keep her body in plaster," he threatened, "until we decide she has become healthy and well." In "Wisdom," Rítsos completes the dictator's simile by smothering a coughing old man from toe to crown: "On the third day we encased him completely in plaster, / leaving only his toothless grin showing." "What possible punishment is he preparing / in his compassion, what retaliation?", the poet wonders in "After a Settlement of Debts." It is now that we must from the beginning "justify the fact that we are still living." It is now that we must endure many deaths, including our own, for there are many ways of dying under such circumstances.

II

We all become involved in the debasement of our own civiliza-
tion, for we have become like those men "Who were amassing
great debts to pay off smaller debts / and spending both these and
those without paying off any." Our words no longer carry weight,
"like down / falling on a mute river after a hunter's gunblast." We
have learned to synchronize our steps with the dead. We begin to
wear one mask after another, at first for disguise and protection
against what we detest and are threatened by; but we must be-
ware and keep alert, for we are in danger of becoming the mask
we use for shield. We profer our disguised gloved hands to be
handcuffed; but the iron clamps may pierce deeper than we know
and cut into our life-veins. Thus, masks can become both a pro-
tection against others and a betrayal against ourselves. Yet at
times we may use them cunningly, to speak through symbolism
and innuendo what is forbidden by censorship, for "the mouths of
the masks always gape open that the other within may speak with
great candor," as the ancient Greek dramatists well know. Those
who can resist the possibility of dangerous identification are only
"the indolent, the thoroughly dead." So long as man is alive and
resists, it is his very vitality that may propel him to the antithesis
of what he once was. All facts, all values become double-faced in
such times of trial. Heroes, both recent and historic, are either
quickly forgotten, dismissed with a few brief speeches, or dis-
torted and exploited by the ruling dictators.

Perhaps as indicative of such impasse as any other poem in this
series is the one that carries for title the dictatorial year during
which these poems were written:

1972

Nights with guns firing and walls. Afterward, quiet.
Scrubbed floors. The chair legs, straight.
Behind the door, a second door and a third; between them
insulating cotton of the kind used to stuff the mouths
of the hungry or the dead. The heroes—he said—
have grown white, dear God, they've grown fat and small.

After the quiet, both appalling and serene, that follows an execu-
tion by firing squad, the charwoman comes to scrub away the
blood. Amid such devastation, where men and ideals go under, it
would seem that even inanimate objects, drenched with blood,

xiii

would also crumple and fall, but the legs of the chair remain firm and straight, a hint that there are men, like those who have been executed, who will remain upright and firm under such trials. There are endless obstacles to be surpassed, one door that opens behind another to infinity, and between each of them the repressive insulating cotton used by all tyrants to prevent the outcries either of the hungry or the dead. Then, suddenly, we are reminded of the very antithesis that may happen amid such scenes of heroism and moral rectitude, for our heroes—either because of their own compromises, or as exploited by ourselves or our leaders, or because we have forgotten them—abruptly grow old, and white-haired and pallid, grow fatter, and lose their stature.

Although Rítsos still keeps his allegiance well within the left-wing movement, he has long since departed from the purely partisan poetry of his youth and has attained a humanistic, mature, and dual view of the world from which he can still condemn and yet understand with compassion that mankind is often caught in traps of its own devising and must be helped to extricate itself, firmly and without malice. We act and are acted upon; men who have become heroes can also, with the erosion of time, circumstance, volition, or simply exploitation, fall from grace and heights maintained only by the most precarious balance. In "Caught in the Act," the poet *knows* that the man seated opposite him, outwardly handsome, scrubbed clean, with dazzling teeth and well-ironed shirt, hides, for all that, a very dirty handkerchief in his pocket. When the man guiltily takes it out and gives it to him with an imploring look, the poet unfolds it, shows it to him empty of any incriminating evidence, then puts it in his own pocket and says to the world at large: "I will not testify against him." We have each in our own way contributed to the world's dirty linen. Let him who is without sin cast the first stone, although not like the pusillanimous man in "Lack of Will Power" who, after being drenched by his tormentors with a rubber hose and flung into a well, rises in spirit voluntarily above the well and himself casts a stone upon himself.

Ritsos's mature view encompasses the disturbing malformations mortals may undergo, and in "Exoneration" embraces with an all-inclusive compassion pederasts, mutes, and even necrophiles, for the protagonist in this poem is suddenly overwhelmed by a startling insight: "How strange — he said — to realize suddenly that no one is to blame," But the compassion that understanding brings for mankind's general plight does not blind Rítsos to the fact that such encompassing exoneration does not in the least preclude the demands of action where one must of necessity narrow principles and resist one's opponents. Thus, in "Opposition," it is the opponent who says, "in an unjustifyingly intense voice," "There's no change, / there's no change without bloodshed," and by such a statement traps *his* opponent in the same relentless net.

A figure of existentialist despair at times, man in *Scripture of the Blind* is faceless, an image of reality. Here mirrors hold the image, multiply it, distort it, partially return it, make it more real than its original, or refuse it altogether. Many of the faces we see are viewed through a window or against it, a suggestion that the face may itself be transparent. Elsewhere identity is equally confused: a woman without a mirror-image appears, as does a nameless coffin; masks, wigs, disguises proliferate; identities are exchanged with blind men, with statues. The reality of a face may be that of a mask, as in "Vulnerability," in which the mask that will not come unstuck becomes the face. Death itself is described as "not having a mirror any longer," implying that life is only death's mirror-image. When the mirror is present, as in "Justice," bullets cannot shatter its reflecting surface; they merely pass through it, leaving holes through which the slain reach out to steal the bread of the living — a two-way mirror from the past to the present, life to death. Human images are less reflections than warning, as in "Inflated Obstacles," a prescience of possibilities, like the pocketed newspaper that the mute customs officials did not read. Yielding to our masks, and to our statues (images again of ourselves), we cease living. Like the old men of "The Statue in the Cafe" — failed actors in makeup and dyed hair who believe a statue depicts their true age — we are frozen in time. Trapped thus between the living and the dead, between identity and facelessness, the protean image explodes, multiplying itself in one instance, dissolving in another.

III

Basically, all of Ritsos's short poems are testimonies and witnesses, as he himself has noted, to fleeting moments of life to which he may respond with lightning speed by pinning them down under a microscope to examine them minutely and thus magnify them into life's awareness, a seizure and arrest of life's unceasing flux. They are also a reaction against the dangers of rhetoric and diffusion that always lurk in ambush behind the writing of a long poem. They are therefore compact and laconic, lack abstraction, crammed with objects and things. Even persons are often seen objectively, unsentimentally, with an almost cruel detachment, as though they were themselves objects also, and their emotions and reactions little different from the movements of wind or waves. Human beings are perceived at times at a dramatist's distance, disinterestedly; yet beneath this seeming detachment the arteries bleed, the heart is lacerated, the mind is torn, the body bruised.

These "objects" play dual and paradoxical roles. Although they are simple, tangible, irrational concretions, things in themselves as they really are, and although human beings may be doubtful of their origins and their destination, they are also the small and innocent accumulators of human emotion and thought that lave them daily and make them the willing and innocent pawns in a drama that really does not concern them. They are called upon, Rítsos writes, "to play the role of 'nothing is happening' when indeed everything is happening." Nevertheless, as "unparticipating mediators," they, their manipulators, and the poet himself, are once again plunged into a worse isolation where no communication is possible. Within them resides the indefinite, the inexplicable, the irresponsible elements of life. They remain incomprehensible, they contain the "enchantment of ambiguity," they raise questions to which there may be no answers.

Take, for example, the shortest of the short poems in this collection, the couplet that comprises "The Mute:"

I permitted the mute to sleep in my bed;
I stole his slippers, put them on, and prayed.

The first ambiguity arises when we are told that the poet *permitted* the mute to sleep in his bed, thus forcing us to raise questions regarding the relationship between poet and mute in which permission for such familiarity must be given and not taken for granted, as between family, friends, or lovers. The permission given is not for the mute simply to repose on the poet's bed but to *sleep* there, thus placing the poet's subsequent actions in a situation where the mute is unaware of what is happening, his muteness deafened in the insularity of sleep. The mystery of their relationship is further heightened when the poet neither borrows nor simply wears the mute's slippers but furtively *steals* them. When the poet then prays, seemingly before the mute on his bed,

xvi

we are not told whether he prays for himself, *for* or *to* the mute, or in regard to some relationship between them. The poet does not, it must be noted, wear the mute's *shoes,* but his *slippers,* and in so doing takes off his own sounding footwear to accept the muffled gait of one enwrapped in silence. Between poet and mute there exists, symbolically, an attraction as between opposites, a mutual concern with silence and sound. In speaking out, the poet breaks silence, and in so doing must struggle to express an insight that in its endeavor for ultimate revelation must strain toward silence. Able to hear but unable to speak, the mute, as poet, is necessarily doomed to a silence that is poetry looking in upon itself. Of the two, it is the poet who is most envious, who kneels and prays to silence in a state of sleep and, perchance, of dream. Together, poet and mute strain for a longed-for and unattainable whole — which is God, it may be — and which man cannot endure.

This by no means exhausts the suggestive possibilities residing in each word, object, or event. We are given no explanations; interpretations inevitably arise in our minds by these juxtapositions and the tensions they provoke. Central, perhaps, is the fact that the poet wears the mute's slippers and then prays, thus suggesting some sort of identification between poet and mute. This *may* be the essential ambiguity and the implied revelation of the poem, and we may permit our imaginations to roam around our own general or private conceptions of what mutes and poets signify; but as in all poets of consequence, individual words such as "mute" carry a weight and suggestivity further enriched and enlightened by their use not only in this particular book — as we shall see — but also in the poet's entire work.

In such poems, however, it is less important for us to try to penetrate into what we think the poet has in mind than to play freely amid the many probabilities inherent in the events as arranged and presented to us by the poet. Yet, if the poet had not himself a powerful and central insight that impelled him to write down these words in exactly this manner, undoubtedly the poem would for us have no resilience or meaningful suggestivity. The depth of our own insight depends on the depth of the poet's own insight, insights less coexistent than coextensive. Furthermore, the poet is always aware that his singular insight contains reverberations with which he is himself as tantalized as his readers, and therefore looks to *us* for further extensions, probabilities, or stimulations that may extend but never exhaust.

Let us consider another poem, "Liturgical":

He placed the paper box on the table quietly
as though it were a closed, uninhabited monastery. For a while
he was gone in the other room. We could hear the faucet run-
     ning—
Perhaps he was washing his hands with soap. On returning,
he opened the box with great care, and placed
his left hand within it. Then with his right hand
he seized his left by the wrist, took it out,
raised it up high, and showed it to us.

We note immediately that the paper box is only *likened* to a
closed, uninhabited monastery, thus investing its *implied* empti-
ness with an aura of probable sanctity. The protagonist then goes
into another room, from which we can hear the faucet running.
Again, in line with suggestivities we have been given, rather than
statements, we are told that *perhaps* (a recurrent word through-
out Rítsos's poetry) he was washing his *hands*. If we keep the title
in mind, the fact that the box was likened to a monastery, and the
subsequent fact that the protagonist's hands become the chief
actors in the drama, we may infer that he had been washing his
hands in an act of ablution, as in ceremonial purification. We then
note that on returning he opens the box with the great care proper
to sacred ritual and into it places not his right, but his *left* hand,
called in Greek folklore, "the heart's hand," imbued with sen-
sitivity and compassion because it lies on the heart's side of the
body. Then with his *right* hand — which lies on the side of the
body where muscular action, in most individuals, is strongest and
therefore the symbol of power and action — he does not simply
take but *seizes* the left hand by the wrist, as though to impede or
at least restrain it. But, on the contrary, we see that the right hand
of action has seized the weaker left member to assist in a gesture
which — perhaps — it was incapable of completing in itself.

What, however, is that which is revealed when the right hand
raises the left hand high and shows *it* to us? Is it the hand itself,
now radiating with whatever it had been immersed in the box, or
does "it" refer, even obliquely, to whatever the hand had brought
out and was holding up to our view, as in the hand — perhaps —
of a priest at the holy altar? We are not told, just as we can never
know what a chalice or wafer may contain, or any other recepta-
cle of sacred mysteries. Indeed, Rítsos himself may be likened to
a closed uninhabited monastery (and therefore inhabited by cen-

turies of sacred and inherited memories) from which his right hand firmly assists his left to raise high for our inspection these fleeting poems he offers us as testimonies. Those of a political slant of mind will no doubt ferret out further innuendoes of "right" and "left." Although in Greece one may speak of a left-handed marriage, or of being born on the left side, that is, on the wrong side, of the blanket, there are other implications of this word in English, not residual in Greek, of clumsiness, awkwardness and insincerity, attributes sometimes associated with what is weak and often compassionate. Conversely, the word "right" in Greek carries connotations of the clever, skillful, dexterous, adroit, and apt, but does not carry the English connotations of the true, just, correct, upright, or lawful. It is well to keep in mind that sometimes in translation a poem may take on reverberations and meanings, for good or ill, not residual in the language in which it was written.

IV

Beyond the questions it raises, *Scripture of the Blind* reveals in Ritsos's work a feeling that poetry is rooted as much in instinct and inspiration as in craft. "Poetry," he writes in "The Meaning of Art," "always begins before the words or after the words." In "There" a woman feels her necklace suddenly becoming weightless "in an intelligible position of studied silence," and it is such isolated and petrified moments, where a detail is caught and framed, that "poetry waits to be discovered." It may be as insignificant a detail as moisture sparkling on the back of a guitar that "prevents the world fron dying," for "wherever I look about me," the poet says in "Rwed Innocence," "at the stairs, the lantern, the nail on the wall, I detect a miracle." Once given shape, the poem is compared, in "The Poem and the Poet," to "a tiger's tongue in the cage." Trapped in a form that both controls and suggests, poetry is likened thereafter to a circus, but one that does not entirely achieve the intended effect; while the poet is not himself deceived, neither does he deceive: the children (our real audience, the uncorrupted within us) do not gather. But Ritsos is not, in this book, exclusively a poet of "deception"; for he is here, as elsewhere in his work, a poet who can still affirm his social purpose. Associating in "Silent Praise" the roles of student, poet, and revolutionary, he claims the superior insights of one who, serving a social function, knows better than anyone else the "secret of the statue."

xix

One finds in *Scripture of the Blind* that which one has sensed in other of Ritsos's recent works, a subtly ironic posture. In "Anonymous Street" a woman finds herself at last ready to reply, but "there was no one there to ask." Again, in "Change of Pace," a shoeblack calls out in the night, "Next", and, involuntarily, the poet changes step as though to synchronize it with that of the dead man. With this irony appears a certain wistfulness, even whimsy. "Vigilance" possesses a certain charm similar to that of Mayakovsky's "A Cloud in Trousers," but, like Mayakovsky, Rítsos treads a suicidal line in his poetry along which whimsy is vastly out of place, if, nevertheless, periodically welcome.

These situations, in human terms, could turn tragic if the poet could not play with objects — things and persons both — at times comically, at times ironically, at times compassionately, but always creatively and dramatically, in terms of disguise and metamorphosis. The unavoidably tragic becomes at times caricature, at times paradox, at times absurdity. What finally matters, what finally emerges, what finally is "real" or "true" is the created poem itself, the redemption of art. That the "poem" almost instantly becomes another innocent "object," another pebble on the endless shores of time, subject to the whims of whoever picks it up to place beneath the microscope of his own interpretive eyes, simply defines the ultimate isolation of all phenomena, the basic tragedy known to every clown or charlatan or poet.

V

In disgussing the specific role that common objects play throughout his poetry, particularly in his short poems, Ritsos once mentioned the word "string." In *Scripture of the Blind,* we read of the red piece of string with which a woman binds her hair; of the piece of string a deaf-mute carries in his pockets and with which he ties a bird's foot; of wet strings from children's kites hanging from trees where they have been snagged; of pieces of string covering up hoops from old barrels; of the string with which the tops of nylon clothing bags are tied, hanging in the closet; of well-waxed strings used by peasant women to sew pieces of cloth or matting over baskets containing morsels of food and personal items to send off, perhaps, to a son in the army. There are even the invisible "strings of night" over which two drunks stumble. Such common, everyday, humble items are steeped in the storehouse of subconscious memory with those fresh, indelible impressions we all receive in childhood when we encounter them for the first time in various situations and from which they take on new auras of association, disguise, and metamorphosis until ultimately they accumulate a myth of their own, shifting, changing, and evoking within us unfathomable accretions.

Although Rítsos referred to "string" as an example of how the simplest objects are redolent with countless associations for man, it is among the lowest in the scale of reference in *Scripture of the Blind*. The "objects" that play a much greater role in the poems are, in descending scale: persons of various ages, professions, and conditions, feet and footwear, invalids of various kinds, fingers and gloves, shops, windows and windowpanes, the naked, stairs, mirrors, things hidden or hiding, statues, dogs, tables, water glasses, sleep, fish, trains and railroad stations; and then, in lesser roles, there are matches, bread, masks, keys, urinals and urinating, baskets, cages, stones, wigs, playing cards, wills.

Even words become objects, lifted out of their abstract definitions in dictionaries to merge in color and contradiction when associated with thousands of emotional reactions apprehended in a thousand different situations. Each object has not only one facet but a million, each revealed according to where it finds itself or has been placed in space and time, and with what or whom. Although it does not change its identity with any other creature or thing, it does change color or aspect by proximity alone, like an octopus, or like the many creatures in nature — plant, animal, mineral — that camouflage themselves or adapt to their environment in order to survive.

This constant transformation of the simplest object in Rítsos's poems imbues them with an aura of mystery inseparable from the mystery of existence itself. They are picked up by human beings, seen, touched, smelled, felt, used, at times abstracted, at times given a symbolical significance foreign to their nature, at times discarded, at times treasured; but beneath the divisionary multiplicity forced upon them, they always bear the gravity of their own undivided integrity. Presented in simple sentence structure, wherein each object is given an undivided attention of utmost clarity, they are, nonetheless, often not related to one another by any surface logic of continuity or plot but are juxtaposed one against the other so abruptly, so unexpectedly, so surprisingly, that the reader is forced to wonder in what way they are related to one another and what the drama is which is being played out between them. They possess both the precision and yet the blurred and symbolical significance of objects seen in dream. We sense they are wearing the masks that their role in any one particular circumstance imparts to them, or the makeup with which we ourselves have chosen to cover them, and this blurs and confuses their relationship and their interreaction with one another. Yet beneath their disguises we feel that their "real" identities are engaged in an interlocked and relentless battle between life and death. They are the contorted images of nightmare, *our* nightmare. The masks they wear are at times comic (in the sense of a Divine Comedy), at times ironic, at times highly fantastic; but the roles they play are at all times tragic and existentialist.

There are two worlds: that of objects outside the human consciousness (including the human body), and the persons who manipulate these objects and are manipulated by them unknowingly. The objects, by their innate gravity, their weight, their integrity, their unique shapes, passively strive to retain their identity, to resist transformation in the hands and minds of mortals, and this is a major part of the drama inherent in these poems. Each object retains its particualr form and color, but like a piece of glass or enamel in a mosaic, it becomes part of a larger pattern of which it has no comprehension, since it is not blended into the other separate objects in merging tones, as in painting, but is isolated from the others like islands by the rigidity of their outlines. English syntax commonly refers to *a* person or thing and thus generalizes, but Greek syntax commonly refers to *the* person or thing, and thus isolates and particularizes. Although this is often transferable in translation into English terms, in Rítsos the specification is so strong that persons and things insist on their particularity, upon being given an identity apart from others. For this reason, in these poems the reader will often find *the* woman, *the* table, *the* water glass and not simply a woman, a table or a water glass. They are the individual and isolated dots of a Braille system that must be read by the groping fingers of all the senses to make out the holy scripture of the blind.

VI

As all dramatists know — and Rítsos is essentially a dramatist — the normality of life can only be invoked by depicting the frustrating and frustrated actions of abnormality. There are over sixty different kinds of living persons in these poems, and half as many dead. Those living on the margins of time better invoke normality by their very eccentricity. They are conjurors, public executioners, deserters, dwarfs, hunchbacks, clowns, oarsmen, refugees from insane asylums, soldiers, sailors, animal trainers, burglars, pederasts, necrophiles, failed actors, money changers, murderers, quilt makers. The dead are firemen, warriors, women, the drowned, the slain, the hanged, the crowned, the refrigerated. In addition, there are a handful of old men and women, a score who are in some way invalid, either rachitic, hydrocephalic, armless, sick, leprous, crippled, paralytic, disabled, and in various ways bandaged. And then, at the very heart of these poems, there are a dozen or so deaf persons, mutes, and deaf-mutes, and many more blind persons as symbols for all the other invalids, physical or mental, who pervade these poems written during the junta years. We are all blinded in some way or another, not only in our eyes but also in our limbs, our hearts, our habits, our relationship to one another. In this sense, these poems are a scripture written *by* the blind *for* the blind.

The deaf, like Beethoven, may hear the inner music of the Last Quartets that almost succeeds in bringing to harmony that tension between dualities Beethoven so dramatized in symphonies when his hearing was acoustically sound and before he heard unheard melodies and piped to Keatsian "ditties of no tune." The mute may attain that inner state for which all poetry strives, the ultimate silence in which lies the perfect Word before creation, and like the poet himself in his poem, contorts his face into distorted caricatures that verge on tearful laughter in an attempt to communicate from beyond the margins of silence. "This, then, which we call loss —" the poet concludes in "Questioning Conclusion," "is it perhaps something added?"

In "The District 'Thimarákis,' 1939," it is the mute who sings; in "At the Harbor's End," it is the deaf-mute who hears the bird of omen croaking; in "Stages of Ignorance," it is the real blind man who sees and snatches away the dark glasses from a man who no longer wants to confront the world of reality after all his supports have been cut off from under him so that he is compelled to close his eyes (perhaps forever) "lest he betray or refute his previous life, / even though he didn't at all know what his life was, or even in general." The mute, the deaf-mute, and the blind play dual and ambiguous roles, at times the victims of this world, at times prophets who see and hear and speak better than those intact in all their senses. All Greek literature, from ancient to

xxiii

modern times, is haunted by the shades of its three Great Blind Men: Homer, Tiresias, and Oedipus. In Milton's phrase, they are the "blind mouths" that have the courage and the insight to utter truths from which men, with all the intensity of their living senses, strive to flee as from some blinding revelation they do not wish, in terror, to confront. So Tiresias, who had lived through seven transformations from woman into man in seven generations, and who had (in one version) been bestowed with insight by Athena, goddess of wisdom, after she had blinded him, could on the one hand prophesy that Narcissos would live to a ripe old age provided that he know himself, yet on the other hand could force Oedipus step by step relentlessly into self-knowledge. So Oedipus, come to self-knowledge, cruelly blinded himself to punish his fate; for though all his sinful acts may be predestined, a man is caught in the trap of his divising, that of free choice under fated circumstances. And so Homer, though blind — or rather, *because* he was blind — saw beyond the evanescent turmoils of men and of gods and plunged into a reality deeper than natural law or mythical dream. And so Rítsos, dazzled as all true poets must be by blinding insights, can say with his deaf-mute in "At the Harbor's End," "with such obscurities I seek to escape the dark," or, in "The Eyes of the Statue," identify with that man who turns into a towering statue and from a mirror in our house stares at us with his enormous eyes, "White, pure white, blind (we call him blind)," having first warned us before his metamorphosis, "that which you make you become."

VII

Full of strange imminence, *Scripture of the Blind* is a world of the monstrous and the strange, a world filled with a vague expectation of the arrival of someone or something. Men wait because they wish to believe once more. Preparing for reappearance, they wait for the wind, the rain. The postman passes by without stopping, while each searches for the word he was about to say, amid intimations of Christ, a blind Homer, an archangel with red wings. Silence is again and again spoken of as most priceless; people are asked to be quiet; the presence of mutes becomes pervasive. There is no need to shout, for no one listens; the mute are mute, perhaps, because no one will hear. Indeed, one is better heard by not speaking. The poet himself, though his mode of expression is language, eschews words as a medium. In such a world, presumably, it is the awaited, the regenerator of the "word," who will both speak and listen.

As men wait, they are swallowed up by the grotesque details of their existence. Sexuality, in "Outline of a Nightmare," is pictured as a monstrously mythical event: a stout woman with six vaginas who rubs against men while dancing, holding between her teeth a butcher's hook from which hangs Apollo's favorite cow. But the monsters of Rítsos's world are merely part of the natural world; the poet does not try to exorcise the deformed as demonic horrors, for he does not view them as nature's unwanted children, her rejects, but as more real, more natural than those commonly considered "whole" or "normal." Perhaps they are more real because they have suffered, perhaps their instincts are more highly prized because they see with greater insight, not so much as a divinely inspired gift but as a dearly won prize. Pressing on the limits of normality, the deformed are depicted largely as bystanders. They rarely do more than report a situation or suffer from it; their lives do not appear to be structured by their own intent but by that which is inflicted upon them. They live through reflected images, as though through a mirror darkly, without self-knowledge.

Normality, like love, like justice, kindness, compassion, truth, are paradisiacal and nonexistent states that can be imagined only ideally through the dark veils of an ever changing reality. Thus, in these poems, by an expert and dazzling manipulation of all the means available to a highly skilled puppeteer, Rítsos pulls the strings of his creatures, animate and inanimate both, so that in meeting with one another, in clashing, in dialogue, in simply passing each other on the street or ignoring one another in a room, they set up within the onlooker reverberation after reverberation of the essential mystery and miracle that is our and their existence. They carry the burden of the unbearable inexplicablility not only of the human but also of total existence. In their dreamlike trance, in their abrupt and unexpected juxtapositions to one another, they seem to be surrealist in origin, but are only so in impact. Beneath their seemingly illogical disconnections the reader-interpreter senses that a logic of the imagination is at play, that beneath the absurdity of their individual existence and their deeds lies the luminous rationale of their creator — luminous because Rítsos, like Kazantzakis, has accepted the ultimate absurdity of life but has pushed far beyond it in gratitude for life's teeming multiplicity in order to embrace all phenomena in a fierce, almost savage, love and affirmation. He would agree with Kazantzakis's Odysseus that "Death is the salt that gives to life its tasty sting."

Kimon Friar
Kostas Myrsiades

ΥΑΛΟΓΡΑΦΙΑ ΛΟΥΤΡΟΥ

Πῶς εἶχε πυκνώσει ὁ ἀέρας ἀπ' τὶς μυρωδιὲς τῶν μύρτων
κι ἀπ' τοὺς πρησμένους ἀτμούς. Κι αὐτὸς κλεισμένος κιόλας
μέσα στὸ δίχτυ, βλέποντας ψηλὰ τὸ παράθυρο. Στὸ θαμπὸ τζάμι
σχεδιασμένο τὸ λευκὸ καμπαναριό. Τὸ σκοινὶ τῆς καμπάνας,
πιθανὸν κρατημένο ἀπ' τὸ μεγάλο ἀόρατο χέρι,
δονήθηκε ἄξαφνα κι ἀντήχησε δοξαστικὸς ὁ ἄτμητος ἦχος
ἀνάμεσα στὶς λάμψεις τῶν σπαθιῶν καὶ στὰ σπασμένα κατάρτια
ἀπ' τὰ καράβια τῆς ἐπιστροφῆς. Τὸ ξέρεις—ψιθύρισε—ἐκεῖνο
ποὺ ἐπιζεῖ τοῦ θανάτου σου εἶναι αὐτὸ ποὺ στερήθηκες στὴ ζωή
σου.

Ἀθήνα, 28.ΙΧ. 72

HYALOGRAPHY OF THE BATH

How much the air had thickened from the myrtle's fragrance
and the swelling steam! And he, already enclosed
within its net, gazing at the high window. The white bell-tower
sketched on the blurred pane. The bell's rope,
probably held by an invisible hand,
suddenly vibrated as the uninterrupted clang reverberated gloriously
between the glittering swords and broken masts
of ships returning. You know it well — he murmured — that
    which survives
your death is that of which you deprived yourself in life.

Athens, 9/28/72

3

ΥΣΤΑΤΗ ΑΘΩΟΤΗΤΑ

Φόρεσε τὰ παπούτσια του, τὰ γάντια του, τὴ σκούφια του.
Ἐσώρρουχα καὶ ροῦχα—τίποτα. Βγῆκε στὸ δρόμο.
Ὁ ὑδραυλικός, ὁ καρβουνιάρης, ὁ χασάπης, ὁ ἀστυφύλακας,
ὁ γέρο-σκύλος μὲ τὴν κομμένη οὐρά, δυὸ σημαῖες,
ἡ μεγάλη κόκκινη γυναίκα στὸν τοῖχο. Πλησίασε,
ἔβγαλε τὸ δεξί του γάντι νὰ τὴ χαιρετήσει. Τότε,
πιέζοντας τ᾽ ἄδειο του γάντι μὲ τ᾽ ἄλλο του χέρι, ἀνακάλυψε
ἐκεῖνο τὸ χαμένο ἀπὸ χρόνια πατρικὸ δαχτυλίδι
κι᾽ εἶδε ταυτόχρονα πὼς εἶταν γυμνὸς κάτω ἀπ᾽ τὸ βλέμμα
τῆς κόκκινης γυναίκας. Δὲν τοῦ ἀπόμενε πιὰ τίποτα.
Ἔβγαλε καὶ τὰ δυὸ παπούτσια του. Ἔβαλε μέσα στὄνα
τὰ γάντια του· στ᾽ ἄλλο τὴ σκούφια του. Κι᾽ ἔτσι μονάχος
χαμογελώντας σὲ μιὰν ὕστατη ἀθωότητα, πρόσφερε
ὁλόγυμνα τὰ χέρια του στὶς χειροπέδες.

Ἀθήνα, 28.IX.72

ULTIMATE INNOCENCE

He put on his shoes, his gloves, his cap.
Underclothing and clothing — none. And he went out into the street.
The plumber, the coal dealer, the butcher, the policeman,
the old dog with its tail cut, two flags,
the large red woman on the wall. Approaching her,
he removed his right glove to greet her. Then,
squeezing the empty glove with his other hand,
he detected that ancestral ring lost years ago,
and at the same time saw himself naked under
the red woman's gaze. Nothing was left him any more.
He then removed both shoes also, placed his gloves
in one of them, his cap in the other. And thus, alone,
smiling in an ultimate innocence, he profered
his naked hands to the handcuffs.

Athens, 9/28/72

ΧΩΡΙΣ ΚΑΘΡΕΦΤΗ ΠΙΑ

Τὰ μαλλιά της πεσμένα στὰ μάτια της, στὸ στόμα της·
μασάει τὰ μαλλιά της· τὸ σάλιο της ἀσπρίζει.
Μεγάλη σκιὰ στὴν κουρτίνα. Τὰ ποτήρια στὸ πάτωμα.
Νὰ τὸ φωνάξεις ὥς τὸ τέλος, ν' ἀντιστρέψεις, νὰ κρύψεις.
Νὰ κρύψεις τί; νὰ κρυφτεῖς ποῦ; «Θάνατος», φώναξε·
«γερατειά, θάνατος», φώναξε. Νὰ φύγω. Κράτησέ με.
Ἕνας λόφος σπαρμένος μὲ θραύσματα ὀβίδων. Κι' ἐκεῖ,
ἀνάμεσα σὲ κόκκαλα, μιὰ χτένα, ἕνας κόκκινος σπάγγος,
νὰ χτενιστεῖς χωρὶς καθρέφτη πιά, νὰ δέσεις τὰ μαλλιά σου
νὰ μὴ σοῦ πέφτουνε στὰ μάτια, μὴ σοῦ κρύψουνε τ' ἄσπρο
    σκουλήκι
ποὺ ἥσυχο, ἀργό, γλοιῶδες ἀνεβαίνει στὸ τραπέζι.

Ἀθήνα, 29.IX.72

WITHOUT A MIRROR NOW

Her hair fallen over her eyes, her mouth,
she chews at her hair; her saliva whitens.
A great shadow on the curtain. The water glasses on the floor.
Shout it until the end; turn it about, hide it.
Hide what? Hide yourself where? "Death!" she shouted.
"Old age, death!" she shouted. I'll run away. Hold me back.
A hill strewn with shell fragments. And there,
amid bones, a comb, a red piece of string,
to comb yourself without a mirror now, to bind your hair
that it might not fall over your eyes, that it might not hide from
    you the white worm
that slimily, serenely, sluggishly crawls up the table.

                                        Athens, 9/29/72

ΠΕΡΙ ΗΡΩΩΝ

Τοὺς συμπαθήσαμε τοὺς ἥρωες, τοὺς λυπηθήκαμε. Πολὺ γρήγορα
τοὺς λησμονᾶμε ἢ τοὺς ξεφορτωνόμαστε μὲ τίποτα λογύδρια
ἢ καὶ τοὺς ἀντικαθιστοῦμε μὲ ἄλλους. «Ἂν ἤξεραν», εἶπε ἡ Μαρία,
«ἂν ἤξεραν ἀπὸ πρίν». Δὲ συνέχισε. Καταλάβαμε. Οἱ πιότεροι
σπρώχνουν ἕνα παλιὸ χειραμάξι μὲ ἔπιπλα σακατεμένα,
μὲ ξεβαμμένες πινακίδες καὶ τίτλους νεκρούς. Οἱ ἄλλοι, τυχερότεροι,
εἶναι ἀπὸ χρόνια σκοτωμένοι—συνηθίσανε στὴ λησμονιά. Τὰ βράδια
μαζεύονται πάνου στὸ πατάρι· δὲ μιλᾶνε· ἀνάβουν τσιγάρο.
Οἱ τρεῖς στὸν παλιὸ καναπέ. Οἱ δυὸ στὶς πολυθρόνες. Ὁ μικρότερος
χάμου στὸ πάτωμα, γλυκὸ παιδί, κυλώντας ἀργὰ τὸ καρούλι
ἐκείνης τῆς μεγάλης ἄδειας κουβαρίστρας. Τὸ καρούλι σκοντάφτει
στὸ πόδι μιᾶς καρέκλας ἢ στὸ μαῦρο παπούτσι τοῦ Βαγγέλη,
ἀλλάζει κατεύθυνση, γυρνάει, σταματάει. Τότε, στὸ διάδρομο κάτω,
ἀκούγεται ὁ ἐλάχιστος θόρυβος τοῦ διακόπτη ὅπως ἀνάβουν τὰ ἔξω
    φῶτα
καὶ φεύγουνε παρέες οἱ καλεσμένοι, διπλωμάτες, στρατηγοί,
    τιτλοῦχοι,
καὶ τελευταῖοι οἱ τρεῖς τυφλοὶ μουσικοί. Μὲς στὰ βιολιά τους
οἱ χαρτοκλέφτες ἔχουν κρύψει τὶς σημαδεμένες τράπουλές τους.

Ἀθήνα, 30.ΙΧ. 72

ON HEROES

We sympathize with heroes, feel sorry for them. Very quickly
we forget them or get rid of them with a few brief speeches,
or even replace them with others. "If they only knew,
if they only knew beforehand," said Maria. But she did not
    continue. We understood.
Most of them push an old wheelbarrow with broken-down furniture,
with faded shop signs and dead titles. Others, much luckier,
were murdered many years ago — they've become inured to
    forgetfulness. In the evenings
they gather up in the loft, don't talk, light a cigarette or two.
Three on the old couch. Two in armchairs. The youngest
down on the floor, a sweet boy, slowly rolling the reel
of that large empty spool of thread. It bumps against
the foot of a chair or Vangélis' black foot,
changes direction, turns, stops. Then in the downstairs corridor
is heard the slight click of the switch as the outside lights go on,
and the invited break up in groups — diplomats, generals, the
    titled,
and last of all the three blind musicians. Inside their violins,
the card sharks have hidden a marked pair of cards.

Athens, 9/30/72

9

ΓΥΜΝΟ ΠΡΟΣΩΠΟ

Νὰ κόψεις τὸ λεμόνι, νὰ ρίξεις δυὸ στάλες στὸ ποτήρι·
νά, τὰ μαχαίρια πλάϊ στὰ ψάρια πάνω στὸ τραπέζι—
τὰ ψάρια εἶναι κόκκινα, τὰ μαχαίρια εἶναι μαῦρα·
ὅλοι μ᾿ ἕνα μαχαίρι στὰ δόντια ἢ στὸ μανίκι, στὴ μπότα ἢ στὸ
    βρακί τους·
οἱ γυναῖκες τρελλάθηκαν, θέλουν νὰ φᾶνε τοὺς ἄντρες,
ἔχουν μεγάλα μαῦρα νύχια· χτενίζουν τ᾿ ἄλουστα μαλλιά τους
ψηλά, ψηλὰ σὰν πύργους ἀπ᾿ ὅπου γκρεμίστηκαν κάτω
ἕνα - ἕνα τὰ πέντε παιδιά· μετὰ κατεβαίνουν τὴ σκάλα,
βγάζουν νερὸ ἀπ᾿ τὸ πηγάδι, πλένονται, ἀνοίγουν τὰ σκέλια,
χώνουν τὰ κουκουνάρια μέσα τους, χώνουν τὶς πέτρες. Ἐμεῖς
κουνᾶμε τὸ κεφάλι: «ναὶ» καὶ «ναί»· κοιτᾶμε χάμου
ἕνα μερμήγκι, μιὰν ἀκρίδα ἢ τὸ ἄγαλμα τῆς Νίκης—
ἐπάνω στὰ φτερά της σεργιανᾶνε οἱ κάμπιες τῶν πεύκων.

Ἡ ἔλλειψη ἁγιότητας—εἶπε—εἶναι ἡ ἔσχατη, ἡ χειρότερη γνώση·
αὐτὴ ἀκριβῶς τὴ γνώση μένει τώρα νὰ ὀνομάσουμε ἁγία.

                                                    Ἀθήνα, 30.IX.72

NAKED FACE

Cut the lemon and let two drops fall into the glass;
look there, the knives beside the fish on the table—
the fish are red, the knives are black.
All with a knife between their teeth or up their sleeves, thrust in
    their boots or their breeches.
The two women have gone crazy, they want to eat the men,
they have large black fingernails, they comb their unwashed hair
high up, high up like towers, from which the five boys
plunge down one by one. Afterward they come down the stairs,
draw water from the well, wash themselves, spread out their thighs,
thrust in pine cones, thrust in stones. And we
nod our heads with a "yes" and a "yes" — we look down
at an ant, a locust, or on the statue of Victory —
pine tree caterpillars saunter on her wings.
The lack of holiness — someone said — is the final, the most
    dreadful knowledge;
it's exactly such knowledge that now remains to be called holy.

Athens, 9/30/72

11

ΔΗΜΟΣΙΟΣ ΛΟΓΟΣ

Πῶς ἔγινε ἔτσι μὲ κεῖνο τὸ τσουβάλι τὰ κάρβουνα
ἀφημένο μπροστὰ στὸν καθρέφτη τῆς εἰσόδου; Πῶς ἔγινε
μ' αὐτὴ τὴ μπακιρένια λεκάνη μὲ τὸ ζεστὸ νερὸ
ὅπου ἔπλυνε τὰ πόδια του ὁ μεγάλος τυφλός; Περάσαν
οἱ κερδοσκόποι, οἱ συμβιβαστικοί, οἱ ἀδιάλλακτοι,
ὁ κουρέας μὲ τὸ ψαλίδι του, νύχτα, πρὶν χρόνια—δὲ θυμᾶμαι·
ἀνέβηκε στὴν ξύλινη ἐξέδρα· «λόγο», τοῦ φώναζαν· «λόγο»·
ἄνοιξε διάπλατα τὸ στόμα· δὲν ἔβγαλε λέξη· κοίταξε πάνω·
ἔκοψε ἕνα κομμάτι ἀπ' τὴ σημαία, τὄχωσε στὸ τσεπάκι του·
φοβόταν νὰ κοιτάξει κάτω τὰ πλήθη· χαμογέλασε·
«λόγο» τοῦ φώναξαν· δὲν ἤξερε ποῦ νὰ τρυπώσει τὰ χέρια του.
Ποιὸς θ' ἀπολογηθεῖ; Ποιὸ τὸ λάθος; Ποιὸς θὰ δώσει
τὴν ἄφεση ἢ τὴν τιμωρία στοὺς τιμωρημένους; «Ἐγώ». Φώναξε.
«Ἐγώ», ξαναφώναξε. «Τί ἐσύ;» τὸν ρωτήσαμε. Αὐτὸς
ἔκοψε τότε τὸ ζερβί του αὐτὶ μὲ τὸ ψαλίδι του καὶ τὄχωσε στὸ
    στόμα του.

Ἀθήνα, 30.IX.72

PUBLIC SPEECH

How did this happen — with that sack of coal
left before the mirror in the entrance hall? How did it happen
with that copper basin filled with warm water
in which the huge Blind Man washed his feet? Here
the speculators, the compromisers, the implacable,
the barber with his scissors passed by at night, years ago — I
    can't remember.
He mounted the wooden platform. "Speech!" they shouted, "speech!"
He opened his mouth wide, but not a word came out. Looking up,
he cut off a piece from the flag, thrust it into his pocket,
afraid of looking down at the crowd, and smiled.
"Speech!" they shouted, but he didn't know where to put his hands.
Who will vindicate himself? What was the error? Who will grant
pardon or punishment to the condemned? "I," he shouted.
"I," he shouted again. "What do you mean, you?" we asked him. Then
with his scissors he cut off his left ear and stuffed it into his mouth.

Athens, 9/30/72

13

ΓΕΝΙΚΗ ΝΟΣΟΣ

Ὅλοι βιάζονται· βιάζονται· ἔχουν πολλὰ κλειδιὰ στὶς τσέπες τους·
τοὺς λείπει ἕνα κουμπὶ ἀπ' τὸ σακκάκι τους ἢ πιὸ μέσα·
κι' ἐγώ, μὴ μὲ κρατᾶς, βιάζομαι, κοντεύει κιόλας μεσημέρι·
μὴ μὲ κρατᾶς σοῦ λέω· πρέπει νὰ πάω στὴν ἄρρωστη μάνα μου·
πρέπει μὲ τὄνα χέρι μου νὰ τῆς κρατήσω ψηλὰ τὸ κεφάλι,
μὲ τ' ἄλλο τὸ ποτήρι τὸ νερό. Στὸ μόνο δέντρο τῆς αὐλῆς, ἔξω,
ἔχουν κρεμάσει τὰ παγούρια τους οἱ τρεῖς ἀδιάντροποι στρατιῶτες—
τὰ βλέπει ἀπ' τὸ κρεββάτι της, ἐκεῖ στὸ παράθυρο· φοβᾶται·
θαρρεῖ πὼς εἶναι κομμένα κεφάλια. Πρέπει νὰ τῆς τὸ ξαναπῶ
«εἶναι παγούρια, παγούρια, παγούρια». Θὰ τῆς φορέσω
τὶς λιωμένες παντόφλες της στ' ἄπλυτα πόδια. Θὰ κάτσω
ἀντίκρυ στὴν καρέκλα καὶ θὰ περιμένω νὰ πεθάνει
προσπαθώντας νὰ ξεχωρίσω πιὸ κάτω, στὸ λιόλουστο δρόμο,
τί νέα διαλαλεῖ ὁ ψευδὸς ἀπογευματινὸς ἐφημεριδοπώλης.
Κι αὐτὴ τὸ ξέρει πὼς βιάζομαι κι ἂς κάνει πὼς κοιμᾶται· ξέρει
πὼς τὸ νερὸ ἔχει ζεσταθεῖ μὲς στὰ παγούρια ποὺ ἐγὼ κρέμασα στὸ
    δέντρο.

                                                            Ἀθήνα, 2.Χ.72

14

GENERAL MALADY

Everyone's in a hurry; they've many keys in their pockets;
a button's missing from their coats or from further inside.
And I — don't hold me back; I'm in a hurry; it's almost noon now;
don't hold me back I tell you: I must go to my sick mother
and hold her head up high with one of my hands,
and a glass of water in the other. On the only tree in the courtyard
    outside
three shameless soldiers have hung their flasks —
she can see them from her bed, there by the window. She's afraid;
she thinks they're amputated heads. I tell her over and over again:
"They're only flasks, flasks, flasks." I'll put
her worn-out slippers on her unwashed feet. I'll sit
on the chair beside her and wait for her to die, trying
to make out what news the stammering newsboy this afternoon
is crying out in the sunwashed street below.
And she knows I'm in a hurry, though she pretends to be asleep.
    She knows
the water has turned warm in the flasks which I myself had hung
    on the tree.

Athens, 10/2/72

ΜΥΣΤΙΚΗ ΕΞΟΔΟΣ

Δάνεια, χρέη, ὑποθῆκες, ἀσχολίες, ἀδικίες,
δουλειές, ἀναδουλειές, κούραση, πολλοὶ ἀστυφύλακες,
οἱ πιότεροι χωρὶς στολή. Γυμνὰ πεζοδρόμια
κάτω ἀπ᾽ τὶς παρελάσεις. Ἕνας ἄνθρωπος ντυμένος
μὲ σκοτεινὸ νερὸ στέκει στὴν πόρτα. Ἐγὼ
τοὺς τᾶπα: δὲ φταίω· δικαιολογήθηκα πάλι καὶ πάλι·
σᾶς ξεγελάει τὸ χρῶμα μου, εἶπα—κόκκινο ὑγείας;
ὄχι, τοῦ πυρετοῦ· σᾶς τ᾽ ὁρκίζομαι· δὲ φταίω, δὲ φταίω·
νά τὸ φεγγάρι μαρμάρινο, ποὺ χάνει βάρος
ἔξω ἀπὸ τὰ δημόσια οὐρητήρια· τόδες κι ἐσύ·
κλείνουν τὰ μαγαζιά· δὲν προφταίνεις πιὰ ν᾽ ἀγοράσεις
μπογιές, χαρτόνια, κόλλες γιὰ τὶς μάσκες—
μαῦρες καὶ κόκκινες μπογιές. Ὁ μόνος τρόπος
γιὰ νὰ ἡσυχάσω κάπως κ᾽ ἐγὼ εἶναι ν᾽ ἀρρωστήσω,
μπροστὰ στὴν πόρτα τοῦ γηροκομείου μὲ τὸ δεμένο σκυλὶ
καὶ μὲ τὸ τρύπιο γάντι τοῦ ἑνὸς ἀπ᾽ τοὺς δύο πεθαμένους.

Ἀθήνα, 2.Χ.72

SECRET EXIT

Loans, debts, mortgages, occupations, injustices,
employments, unemployments, weariness, many policemen,
most of them not in uniform. Naked pavements
under the parades. A man dressed
in murky waters stands in a doorway. I
told them: I'm not to blame; I was vindicated over and over again.
Is it my color that deceives you, I said — a healthy red?
No, it's a feverish red. I swear I'm not to blame, I'm not to blame.
Look at the marble moon losing weight
outside the public urinals; you saw it too;
the shops are closing; you won't have time now to buy
paints, cardboard, glue for the masks —
black and red paints. The only way
for me to rest a bit also is to fall sick
before the door of the Old Men's Home with the chained dog
and the torn glove that belongs to one of the two dead men.

Athens, 10/2/72

ΣΟΦΙΑ

Αὐτὸ ποὺ εἶταν βουνὸ κ' ὕστερα ἀγέρας κ' ὕστερα ἄστρο·
κ' ἐκεῖνος ποὺ εἶπε «εὐχαριστῶ»—τὅπε σιγὰ μὴν ἀκούσουν
οἱ δυὸ κι ὁ τρίτος, γιατὶ 'ταν πολὺ θυμωμένοι· πετοῦσαν
ἀπ' τὸ παράθυρο κάτω τὰ παπούτσια τους, τ' ἀνθοδοχεῖα,
τοὺς δίσκους τοῦ γραμμόφωνου, ποτήρια, πετσέτες,
γιὰ νὰ θυμώσουμε κι' ἐμεῖς, γιὰ νὰ τοὺς ποῦμε «μή»,
νἄχουν μιὰ πρόφαση γιὰ κεῖνο ποὺ εἶχαν κάνει κιόλας.
Στὸ διπλανὸ δωμάτιο μὲ τὸ μεγάλο σιδερένιο κρεββάτι
ἀκούγεται ὁ βήχας τοῦ γέρου ποὺ πάνω στὴν κουβέρτα
ἔχει ἀποθέσει τὸ μικρὸ βατράχι, καί, μερόνυχτα τώρα,
ἤσυχος, νηστικός, ἐκστατικός, κοιτάει, μελετάει,
τὸ μαλακὸ μηχανισμὸ τῶν πηδημάτων τοῦ βατράχου.
Ὕστερα πιὰ δὲ βήχει. Τὸν ἀκοῦμε ποὺ πηδάει στὸ κρεββάτι.
Τὴν τρίτη μέρα τὸν βάλαμε ὁλόκληρον στὸ γύψο
ἀφήνοντας ἀπ' ἔξω μόνο τὸ φαφούτικο χαμόγελό του.

'Αθήνα, 2.X.72

WISDOM

What was a mountain and afterward air and later a star;
and he who said "Thank you" — said it softly so that
neither the two nor the third might hear it, because they were
    very angry;
they were throwing their shoes out of the window, their flower pots,
their gramophone records, their water glasses and their napkins
that we might get angry too, that we might shout at them "Don't!"
and thus give them an excuse for what they'd already done.
In the room next door with its large iron bed
we can hear the old man coughing; on his blanket
he has placed a small frog, and for days and nights now,
calm, fasting, ecstatic, he stares at and studies
the soft mechanisms of the frog's leaping.
Afterward he stops coughing. We hear him jumping on the bed.
On the third day we encased him completely in plaster,
leaving only his toothless grin showing.

                                    Athens, 10/2/72

ΑΝΕΚΠΛΗΡΩΤΗ ΥΠΟΣΧΕΣΗ

Δῶσ' μου—ἔλεγε—τὴν ἥσυχη, καλὴ ὑπομονή. Δῶσ' μου
ἐκεῖνο τὸ παλιὸ λαδοφάναρο τοῦ ὑπόγειου. Ἡ ἀράχνη
ἀνηφορίζει στὸν τοῖχο. Ἡ σκιά της μεγαλώνει πολύ.
Τὴν κοιτάζω στὰ μάτια. Δὲ μὲ φοβᾶται. Μοῦ δίνει
τὴν πιὸ μακριὰ κλωστή της. Ράβω τὸ φόρεμά μου. Βλέπω:
αὐτὴ ἡ κλωστὴ δὲ ράβει· ξηλώνει. Ἔτσι ἀπομένω
ὁλότελα γυμνὴ μὲ τὸ μικρὸ λαδοφάναρο, μ' ἕνα κουτὶ σπίρτα,
μ' ἕνα μονάχα σκουλαρίκι, ἀποκλεισμένη γύρω-γύρω
ἀπ' τὰ μαχαίρια ποὺ εἶχα ρίξει πρὶν χρόνια στὸ πηγάδι
κι ἀπ' τὰ πέντε τεράστια λυκόσκυλα τοῦ μαλλιαροῦ κρεοπώλη.
Τὰ τρία σκυλιὰ μοῦ σβῆσαν τὸ φανάρι. Τ' ἄλλα δύο
μοῦ βρέξανε τὰ σπίρτα. Δὲν ἀνάβουν. Κ' εἶχα ὑποσχεθεῖ
νὰ φέξω στὴν τυφλὴ ζητιάνα μὲ τὴν κούκλα, ν' ἀνέβει τὴ σκάλα.

'Αθήνα, 3.Χ.72

20

UNFULFILLED PROMISE

Give me — she used to say — a calm, good forbearance. Give me
that old oil lamp from the basement. The spider
crawls up the wall. Its shadow grows enormous.
I look it in the eyes. It's not afraid of me. It gives me
its longest thread. I sew my dreams. But I see
that this thread won't work. It unstitches. And so I remain
completely naked with the small oil lamp and a single box of matches,
with a single earring only, hemmed in round about
by knives I had thrown years ago into the well
and by the hairy butcher's enormous wolf-hounds.
Three of the hounds extinguished the lamp. The other two
pissed on the matches. They won't light up. And I had promised
to light the way upstairs for the old blind beggar woman with the doll.

Athens, 10/3/72

21

ΑΒΟΥΛΙΑ

Ἐκεῖ ποὺ πήγαινε νὰ κοιμηθεῖ στὸν κῆπο, ὀρθός, μὲ τὴ ράχη
στὸ δέντρο,
(ἄκουγε κιόλας μέσα του τὸ μακρινὸ βουητὸ τῆς λιακάδας)
τὴ στιγμὴ ποὺ πλησίαζε ν' ἀγγίξει μὲ τὄνα του δάχτυλο τὴν
ἡσυχία,
τὸν καταβρέξαν ὁλόκληρο μὲ τὸ μακρὺ λαστιχένιο σωλήνα.
Αἰσθάνθηκε
πῶς πρέπει νὰ χαμογελάσει ἢ νὰ θυμώσει. Δὲν μποροῦσε.
Ξαναέκλεισε τὰ μάτια.
Τὸν σήκωσαν ἀπ' τὶς μασκάλες καὶ τὰ πόδια. Τὸν ρίξαν στὸ πηγά-
δι. Αὐτὸς
ἄκουσε κάτου τὸ γδοῦπο τοῦ νεροῦ κι' ἔρριξε ἀπὸ πάνω μιὰ πέτρα.

Ἀθήνα, 4.Χ.72

LACK OF WILL POWER

Just as he was falling asleep, standing upright in the garden with
his back against a tree,
(he could hear within himself already the distant roar of the sunlight)
at the moment he was about to touch serenity with one of his
   fingers,
they drenched him through and through with a long rubber hose.
   He felt
he should smile or become angry. But he couldn't. He closed his
   eyes again
They picked him up by his armpits and his feet. The flung him into
   the well. And he
heard the thump on the water below, and from above cast down a
   stone.

Athens, 10/4/72

23

ΕΞΑΙΡΕΣΗ ΧΩΡΙΣ ΣΗΜΑΣΙΑ

Ἀναποφάσιστα αἰσθήματα, κινήσεις, γεγονότα. Τὸ βράδι
εἶχε ἕνα κίτρινο χρῶμα σὰν ἕνα ποτήρι λεμονάδα
ποὺ πίνει ὁ τυφλὸς μπροστὰ στὸ παράθυρο. Ἐκεῖνος
δὲν ἤξερε ποῦ νὰ πατήσει—στὸ χαλί; στὰ πλακάκια; Τοῦ τὄπα:
θὰ πεθάνεις κ' ἐσύ. Δὲ μὲ πίστεψε. Τώρα οἱ γυναῖκες
γερνᾶνε μονομιᾶς. Δὲν καλοβλέπουν. Τρυποῦν τὸ δάχτυλό τους
μὲ τὴ μεγάλη βελόνα, ὅπως μπαλώνουν, καθισμένες στὸ κρεββάτι,
μιὰ στρατιωτική, πολὺ μακριά, βαμμένη χλαίνη. Στέκουν,
βυζαίνουνε τὸ δάχτυλό τους, ἀποροῦν, κοιτοῦν τὴν καρέκλα,
κοιτοῦν τὴν κουρτίνα νὰ τοὺς πεῖ. Χάνουν καὶ τὴ βελόνα· φοβοῦνται
μὴ καὶ μπηχτεῖ στὰ μεριά τους, στὸν ὕπνο τους. Μόνον ἐγὼ
ποὺ τὄξερα—λέει—ἀπὸ πρίν, μόνον ἐγὼ εἶμαι νέος.

                                                    Ἀθήνα, 5.Χ.72

MEANINGLESS EXCEPTION

Irresolute feelings, movements, events. The evening
was the color of yellow, like a glass of lemonade
drunk by the blind man before the window. He didn't
know where he should step — on the rug, on the tiles? I told him:
You too will die. He didn't believe me. Women now
age abruptly. They don't see well. Seated on a bed,
they pierce their fingers with a large needle as they mend
a very long dyed army coat. They stand up
sucking their fingers, bewildered, looking at the chair,
at the curtain, for an explanation. They even lose the needle, are
    afraid
lest it pierce into their thighs, their sleep. Only I
who have known this long before — he says — only I am young.

Athens, 10/5/72

ΑΥΤΟ ΠΟΥ ΑΚΟΥΓΕΤΑΙ ΠΑΝΤΑ

Μέρα τἠ μέρα πιὸ μόνος, πιὸ μειλίχιος. Δὲ βγαίνει. Κοιτάει
ἀπ' τὸ παράθυρο τὰ μαγαζιά, τ' ἀνθοπωλεῖο, τὸ σκυλί. Δὲ βλέπει.
Ἔχει μιὰν ἔκφραση κουφοῦ ποὺ κάνει τάχατε πὼς ἔχει ἀκούσει,
κι ὅλοι τὸ ξέρουν, ὅπως κι ὁ ἴδιος, μιὰ καὶ μιλάει πιὸ δυνατὰ
ἐκεῖ ἀκριβῶς ποὺ δὲν πρέπει καθόλου. Τὸ χαμόγελό του
γίνεται τότε πιὸ περίλυπο, πιὸ ἠλίθιο, πιὸ βαθύ· τὸ τυλίγει
μὲ προσοχὴ στὸ τρύπιο τσιγαρόχαρτο· τ' ἀφήνει στὸ νιπτήρα,
σ' ἐκεῖνον τὸ μαρμάρινο νιπτήρα τοῦ παλιοῦ σπιτιοῦ του. Ὡστόσο,
τῇ νύχτα, ἔξω ἀπ' τὴν πόρτα μας, πρῶτος αὐτὸς εἶναι ποὺ ἀκούει
τὸ γυμνὸ βρέφος ποὔχουν παρατήσει μέσα στῇ μεγάλη ἀρβύλα.

                                                    Ἀθήνα, 5.Χ.72

26

THAT WHICH IS HEARD ALWAYS

Day by day more alone, more gentle. He doesn't go out. He looks
out of the window at stores, at the flower shop, the dog. He
    doesn't see.
He wears the expression of a deaf man pretending to have heard,
and all know this, even he himself, and yet he speaks louder
precisely where he shouldn't have spoken at all. His smile
then becomes more sorrowful, more idiotic, more profound; he
    wraps it
carefully in torn cigarette paper and leaves it on the wash-stand,
on the marble wash-stand of his old house. And yet,
at night, he is the first to hear, outside our door,
the naked baby abandoned in a large army boot.

                                        Athens, 10/5/72

27

ΣΤΑΘΜΟΣ ΑΓΙΟΥ ΝΙΚΟΛΑΟΥ

Φεύγουν ἕνας - ἕνας μέσα στὴν ψιχάλα. Μόλις ἀνέβουν
τὰ ἑφτὰ σκαλοπάτια τοῦ Σταθμοῦ, στρέφουν γιὰ λίγο τὸ κεφάλι
σὰ νἆναι πιὰ νὰ μὴν ξαναγυρίσουν ἢ σὰ νἄχουν ξεχάσει
στὸ προηγούμενο τραῖνο τὴν ὀμπρέλα τους. Ὕστερα
μένουν στὸν ἀέρα τὰ λαμπιόνια μὲ τὶς στάλες· μένει ὁ ἦχος
ἀπὸ τροχοὺς ποὺ πέρασαν ἐδῶ καὶ χρόνια σὲ μουσκεμένες ράγιες
καὶ κάτι χαλαρό, ἀποκρεμάμενο καθὼς τὸ στόμα τοῦ μεθυσμένου
ποὖκανε λάθος στὴν πόρτα του καὶ μπῆκε βλαστημώντας
στὸ ξένο σπίτι, νιώθοντας αἰφνίδια νὰ βαραίνουν τὰ παπούτσια του
ἀπ᾽ τὴν πολλὴ τὴ λάσπη, χωρὶς νὰ μπορεῖ νὰ ξεμεθύσει.

Ἀθήνα, 5.Χ.72

ST. NICHOLAS STATION

They leave one by one in the drizzle. As soon as they ascend
the station's seven steps, they turn their heads a little,
as though they were never to return or had forgotten
their umbrellas on the last train. Afterward,
the electric globes remain in the air bedewed with rain; the sound
  remains
of wheels that passed by here years ago on drenched rails,
and something loose and dangling like the mouth of that drunk
who mistook his own door and entered swearing into
the wrong house, feeling weighed down suddenly
by his mud-caked shoes, unable to sober up.

Athens, 10/5/72

ΜΟΥΓΓΟ

"Αφησα τὸν μουγγὸ νὰ κοιμηθεῖ στὸ κρεββάτι μου·
τοὖκλεψα τὶς παντόφλες του, τὶς φόρεσα, καὶ προσευχήθηκα.

Ἀθήνα, 6.Χ.72

MUTE

I allowed the mute to sleep in my bed;
I stole his slippers, put them on, and prayed.

Athens, 10/6/72

ΥΠΟΨΙΕΣ

Τὸ δείλι τὰ παιδιὰ εἶναι μόνα μὲ τ' ἀγκάθια καὶ τὶς πέτρες.
Τὰ παιδιὰ εἶναι γερόντια. Τὰ φωνάζουν ἀπ' τὴν πόρτα,
τὰ φωνάζουν ἀπ' τὴν αὐλή. Δὲν ἀπαντᾶνε. Ἡ μάνα τους
εἶναι ἔγκυος πάλι. Ὁ πατέρας λείπει τὰ βράδια. Τὸ ξέρουν—
οἱ πεθαμένοι φορᾶνε ἄσπρα πουκάμισα, καλὰ παπούτσια,
ὅμως στὶς τσέπες τους λιώνουν τὰ εἰσιτήρια τῶν λεωφορείων
κ' ἕνα εἰσιτήριο θεάτρου. Ἥσυχα σύννεφα περνᾶνε
χαμηλὰ στὸ μαῦρο χορτάρι. Τὸ δέντρο ξεράθηκε.
Ἐπάνω στὴ σοφίτα φάνηκε ὁ μικρὸς ταχυδακτυλουργός·
τίναξε τὴν πετσέτα του κ' ἔκλεισε τὰ παντζούρια. Ἀντίκρυ,
στὴν κάμαρα μὲ τὶς κόκκινες κουρτίνες, ἡ γυναίκα
κρύβει τὰ δεκανίκια τοῦ ἀναπήρου κάτω ἀπ' τὰ σεντόνια,
παίρνει τὴ χτένα της, χτενίζεται γρήγορα, γνωρίζοντας
πῶς κείνη τὴ στιγμὴ ἀκριβῶς γυρίζει σπίτι του ὁ εἰσαγγελέας.

Ἀθήνα, 6.Χ.72

32

SUSPICIONS

At dusk the children remain alone with thorns and stones.
The children are old men. They are called from doors,
from courtyards. They don't answer. Their mothers
are pregnant again.Their fathers are away all night. They know it —
the dead wear white shirts, good shoes,
but in their pockets a single theater ticket
and several bus tickets disintegrate. Tranquil clouds pass
low on the dark grass. The tree has withered.
High up in the attic, the young conjurer appears,
shakes his towel and closes the window shutters. Opposite,
in the room with red curtains, the woman
hides the invalid's crutches under the bedsheets,
takes up her comb, brushes her hair hurriedly, realizing
how at that moment exactly the public prosecutor is returning home.

Athens, 10/6/72

ΣΤΗΝ ΙΔΙΑ ΣΥΝΟΙΚΙΑ

Ποῦ νὰ πᾶς τέτοιαν ὥρα· μεῖνε μαζί μου. ᾿Όπου νἆναι θ᾿ ἀκούσουμε
τὶς βραδινὲς καμπάνες—ἀκούγονται ἀπὸ δῶ· κ᾿ ἴσως γι᾿ αὐτὸ
ἕνα κοπάδι μέλισσες καὶ σφῆκες βγαίνουν ἄξαφνα ἀπ᾿ τὴν κάμαρα
τοῦ γέρο - κηροπλάστη. Τὸ μικρὸ χαρτοπωλεῖο ποὺ ἀγοράζαμε
τσιγάρα, χαρτοφάκελα, ἀσπιρίνες, ἔχει κλείσει. Στὸν ἀέρα
ἀπὸ στιγμὴ σὲ στιγμὴ θὰ τιναχτεῖ μιὰ κραυγὴ καὶ θὰ σβήσει
προτοῦ προφτάσεις κἂν νὰ τὴν ἀκούσεις. ῾Ωστόσο τὸ ξέρεις: ὁ τυφλὸς
μετακινεῖ τὶς καρφίτσες του πάνω στὸ χάρτη. Αὐτὲς τὶς καρφίτσες
τοῦ τὶς χάρισε ἡ ἀπέναντι ράφτρα. ᾿Εσὺ καπνίζεις μ᾿ ἕναν τρόπο
σὰ νἄχεις ξεχασμένο ἕνα πουλὶ στὸ κλουβὶ τοῦ διαδρόμου. Καὶ τώρα
θὰ πρέπει ἀπ᾿ τὴν ἀρχὴ νὰ βροῦμε δικαιολογητικὰ ποὺ ἀκόμη ζοῦμε.

᾿Αθήνα, 6.Χ.72

34

IN THE SAME QUARTER

Where can you go at this hour? Stay with me. Soon we shall hear
the evening bells — they can be heard from here; perhaps this is why
a swarm of bees and wasps flies out of the old
candle-maker's room. The small stationery shop, where we bought
cigarettes, envelopes, aspirin, has closed. From moment to moment
a cry tears through the air and vanishes
before you have even time to hear it. Nevertheless, you know
     that the blind man
moves his pins on the map, those pins
given to him by the seamstress next door. You smoke in such a way
as though you'd forgotten and left a bird caged in the corridor.
     And now
we must from the beginning justify the fact that we are still living.

Athens, 10/6/72

ΣΕΜΝΑ ΤΕΧΝΑΣΜΑΤΑ

Ἐκείνη, πάντα ἡ ἴδια, κίνησή του—διόλου νευρική—μιὰ κίνηση
ἁπλή, διακριτικὴ κι ἀργή, σὰ νὰ σκουπίζει τὰ γυαλιά του
μὲ τὴν ἄκρη τοῦ σακκακιοῦ του, ἐνῶ ποτὲ δὲν τὸν εἴδαμε
νὰ φοράει γυαλιά. Κοιτάζει κάτω ἕνα χνούδι, λίγη στάχτη,
ἕνα μικρὸ κομμάτι καφετιὰ κλωστή. Στὸ παράθυρο
πυκνό, θορυβῶδες γαλάζιο. Αὐτὸς ὑποκρίνεται
πὼς δὲν τὸ ἀκούει, ὑποχρεώνοντάς μας ἔτσι
νὰ τ᾽ ἀκούσουμε πολλαπλάσια ἐμεῖς. Ὕστερα
τὸν βλέπουμε νὰ στέκει ἀπέναντί μας, κάπως πλάϊ,
ὅπως αὐτὸς πού, τὴ στιγμὴ ἀκριβῶς ποὺ τὸν ρωτοῦν,
ἔχει ξεχάσει ὁλότελα τὸν ἀριθμὸ τοῦ τηλεφώνου του, καὶ μένει
μετέωρος πάνω ἀπ᾽ τὸ πηγάδι ὅπου σπιθίζουνε τὰ μάτια τῆς τρελλῆς.

                                                          Ἀθήνα, 7.X.72

36

MODEST CONTRIVANCES

That movement of his, always the same — not nervous at all — a movement
simple, discreet, and slow, as though he were wiping his glasses
with the edge of his coat, although we have never seen him
wearing glasses. He looks down at a bit of fluff, a few ashes,
a small piece of brown thread. At the window,
a dense, noisy blue. He pretends
not to have heard it, thus obliging us to hear it
greatly multiplied. Afterward we see him
standing opposite us, somewhat to the side,
like one who, at exactly the moment he is asked,
has completely forgotten his telephone number and remains
hovering above the well where the eyes of the mad woman glitter.

Athens, 10/7/72

ΜΟΝΟΛΟΓΟΣ Μ' ΕΝΑΝ ΚΡΥΜΜΕΝΟ

Ἔνιωσε τὸ τρύπημα στὴν πλάτη. Γύρισε ἀπότομα. Τὸν εἶδε.
Εἶταν κρυμμένος πίσω ἀπ' τὸ δέντρο. Ἡ μιά του μπότα
πρόβαινε μαύρη· γυάλιζε στὸν ἥλιο. Ἐσὺ δὲν εἶσαι;—τοῦ εἶπε·—
ἐσὺ δὲ μάζεψες τὰ πουλιὰ ἀπ' τὸ δάσος; Ξέρω τὸ γήπεδο
μὲ τὶς χιλιάδες κλουβιά, μὲ τὶς χιλιάδες τ' ἀνάκατα παπούτσια
ἀντρικά, γυναικεῖα, παιδικά, γεροντικά. Κάθε νύχτα
βγαίνουν ἐκεῖ οἱ γριὲς ἀπ' τὸ Ψυχιατρεῖο. Κάθονται χάμου
ξεδιαλέγουν παπούτσια γιὰ τὰ πόδια τους, τὰ χέρια τους· ἄλλες
στριμώχνουν τὸ κεφάλι τους στὶς ψηλὲς μπότες τῶν δορυφόρων,
γρυλλίζουν, τρεχλίζουν στὸ σκοτάδι, τυφλές, σάμπως νὰ περπατᾶνε
ἀνάποδα, πατώντας μ' ἕνα ξένο, κούφιο, παράλυτο πόδι
στὸ χαμηλὸ οὐρανὸ κατάσπαρτον μ' ἀγρυπνισμένες κάργιες.

Ἀθήνα, 8.Χ.72

MONOLOGUE WITH SOMEONE HIDDEN

He felt the drilling in his back, turned sharply, and saw him,
saw him hiding behind a tree, one of his black boots protruding
and shining in the sun. Are you or aren't you the one — he said —
the one who gathered the birds from the forest? I know the field
with its thousands of cages, its thousands of jumbled shoes —
men's, women's, children's, old people's. Every evening
the old women from the Insane Asylum go there. They squat on
    the ground
picking out shoes for their feet, their hands; some of them
cram their heads into the high boots of spearmen,
grunting and staggering in the darkness, blind, as though they
    were walking
upside down, stepping with a strange, hollow, paralytic foot
on a low sky completely strewn with vigilant crows.

Athens, 10/8/72

ΑΒΕΒΑΙΕΣ ΥΠΟΧΡΕΩΣΕΙΣ

Αὐτὴ ἡ πρωϊνὴ ἀπροθυμία·—κοιτάζεις κάτω τὸ δρόμο·
οἱ ἄνθρωποι βιάζονται· δὲ βλέπουν δυὸ μέτρα μπροστά τους,—
μισοὶ στὸν ἀέρα, μισοὶ μέσα τους ἢ μέσα στὸν τοῖχο·
σκοντάφτει ὁ τοῖχος στὸν τοῖχο—ἦχος δὲ βγαίνει.
Τὸ ξεσκονόπανο πιάστηκε στὸ δέντρο. Ἔχασα—λέει—
καὶ τὰ πέντε κλειδιά μου. Ὁ ἄλλος κοιτάει τὸν ποδηλάτη.
Ὁ τρίτος μπῆκε στὸ στιλβωτήριο. Ὁ τέταρτος θὰ πέσει
μπροστὰ στὸ φτωχὸ ἐπιπλοποιεῖο. Ὁ πέμπτος
τυλίχτηκε σὲ τρεῖς ἐφημερίδες. Ἐσὺ νὰ τοὺς μαζέψεις·—
πρέπει νὰ νοιαστεῖς γιὰ τὰ φέρετρα· πρέπει νὰ τοὺς βρεῖς
τ᾽ ἀληθινό τους ὄνομα—ἕνα ὄνομα·—ἀλλιῶς τί θὰ μείνει
ἀπ᾽ τὴ μεγάλη πινακίδα σου, φιλόδοξε ἀρχιτέκτονα,—
ἄσπρη, μὲ κόκκινα γράμματα, πάνω ψηλὰ κρεμασμένη
στὸν ἕβδομο ὄροφο τῆς νέας τζαμένιας πολυκατοικίας;
Καὶ τί θὰ μείνει ἀπὸ σένανε ποὺ ἔκοψες μὲ τὸ ἀρχαῖο ψαλίδι
τὰ πέντε σου δάχτυλα, γιὰ νὰ πιστέψουν στὸ ἀτεμάχιστο, καὶ νὰ
  πιστέψεις;

Κάλαμος, 8.X.72

40

UNCERTAIN OBLIGATIONS

This morning reluctance—you gaze on the street below;
people are in a hurry, they can't see five feet before them—
half in the air, half inside themselves or inside the wall;
wall bumps against wall—not a sound emerges.
A dust rag caught in a tree. I lost—he says—
all five of my keys. The other man looks at the cyclist.
The third enters the shoe shine parlor. The fourth will fall
before the cheap furniture store. The fifth
wrapped himself in three newspapers. You must gather them up;
you must take care of the coffins; you must find
their real name—one name—otherwise what will remain
from your large sign, ambitious architect—
white, with red letters, hanging high up
on the seventh floor of the new glass apartment building?
And what will remain of you who with an ancient pair of scissors
    cut off
your five fingers that all may believe in the indivisible, and that
    you may believe?

                                        Kálamos, 10/8/72

ΚΑΤΕΔΑΦΙΣΜΕΝΑ ΚΑΤΑΦΥΓΙΑ

Καὶ τί νὰ κάνεις πιὰ μὲ τοὺς ἀνθρώπους; Τί νὰ κάνεις μὲ τὸ θάνατο;
Τ' ἄπλυτα πιάτα βουνὸ στὴν κουζίνα. Τὰ ποντίκια γλείφουν τὰ πιάτα.
Οἱ γάτες τρῶνε τὰ ποντίκια. Τὰ σκυλιὰ τρῶνε τὶς γάτες.
Οἱ ἄνθρωποι τρῶνε τὰ σκυλιὰ καὶ τοὺς ἀνθρώπους. Τὸ βράδι
φοράει εἰκοσιδύο προσωπίδες. Τὰ περίπτερα κλείνουν. Ἐσὺ
ἀνεβαίνεις τὴ σκάλα, σκάβεις τὸν τοῖχο, βγάζεις τὸν καθρέφτη·
φορᾶς τὴ μεγάλη περούκα· κρεμᾶς στὴ μύτη σου τὸ σκουλαρίκι·
τραβᾶς τὸν κρίκο ψηλά· κρέμεσαι ἀπ' τὸ ἴδιο σου τὸ χέρι·
ἀπὸ κάτω περνάει ὁ κλειδοῦχος μὲ τὸ κόκκινο φανάρι· τότε
βρίσκεις μιὰ πρόφαση· παραμερίζεις, σκύβεις λίγο καὶ ρίχνεις
μὲς στὸ καπέλο τοῦ ζητιάνου τ' ἄδεια φυσίγγια καὶ τὰ δυὸ τὰ γεμάτα.

Κάλαμος, 8.X.72

DEMOLISHED SHELTERS

And what can one finally do with men? What can one do with death?
The unwashed dishes piled mountain high in the kitchen. Mice
  lick the plates.
Cats eat the mice. Dogs eat the cats.
Men eat the dogs and the men. The evening
wears twenty-two masks. The kiosks close. You
climb up the stairs, dig in the wall, take out the mirror,
put on the large wig, hang an earring on your nose,
draw the clasp up high and hang down by your hand.
Below you the switchman goes by with his red lantern. It's then
you find an excuse, step aside, lean down a little and into the
  beggar's hat
cast the empty cartridges and two loaded ones.

                                        Kálamos, 10/8/72

ΣΤΗΝ ΑΚΡΗ ΤΟΥ ΛΙΜΑΝΙΟΥ

Ὁ κωφάλαλος κουνοῦσε τὰ χέρια του,—δὲν ἔκρυβε τὸ φόβο του·
ἔδειχνε κάπου ψηλὰ μὲς στὴ νύχτα. Κανένας δὲν πρόσεχε. Αὐτὸς
εἶχε ἀκούσει τὸν κρωγμὸ τοῦ ἄγριου πουλιοῦ, αὐτὸς μονάχα,
πάνω ἀπ' τὶς καρβουναποθῆκες. Ὅταν ἔβγαλαν ἀπ' τὸ καράβι
τὰ πέντε φέρετρα, ὁ κωφάλαλος κατέβασε τὰ χέρια του, ξετρύπωσε
ἕνα κομμάτι σπάγγο ἀπ' τὴν τσέπη του κ' ἔδεσε τὸ πουλὶ ἀπ' τὸ πόδι.

(Μὲ τέτοιες συσκοτίσεις—λέει—ἐπιζητῶ νὰ διαφύγω τὸ σκοτάδι).

Ἀθήνα, 9.Χ.72

44

AT THE HARBOR'S EDGE

The deaf-mute was waving his hands — he didn't hide his fear —
and pointing somewhere high up in the night. No one paid him
   any attention. But he,
only he, had heard the croak of the wild bird
above the coal bins. When they carried the five coffins
out of the ship, the deaf-mute put his hands down, fished out
a piece of string from his pocket, and tied the bird by one of its feet.

(With such obscurities — he says — I seek to escape the dark.)

Athens, 10/9/72

ΥΠΟΤΡΟΠΗ

Ἂν πιάσει ἀγέρας, ἂν πιάσει βροχή,—σώπα ν᾽ ἀκούσω·
στὸ διπλανὸ δωμάτιο εἶναι ἡ ζυγαριὰ τοῦ μαιευτηρίου·
ἀπ᾽ ἔξω οἱ ξερὲς καλαμποκιές. Κάποιος πέρασε,—δὲν πέρασε;
Παρατηρεῖς τὰ ζυγωματικὰ τῆς νύχτας—προτεταμένα·
ἀκοῦς τὸ τρίξιμο τῶν μεγαλύτερων φύλλων. Μὲς ἀπ᾽ τὶς διακοπὲς
παραμονεύεις τὴ διάρκεια. Πὲς κάτι—ὄχι ἀντίθετο ὅμως.
Δὲ σοῦ τὸ κρύβω: θέλω νὰ πιστέψω πάλι. Ἂν δεῖς πὼς κοιμᾶμαι
σκούντησέ με στὸν ὦμο νὰ ξυπνήσω—χειρότερος ὁ ὕπνος.
Τὸ σφύριγμα τοῦ τραίνου μ᾽ ἄφησε ὁλομόναχο μέσα σὲ τοῦτο τὸ
    σπίτι
κατοικημένο ἀπ᾽ τοὺς πνιγμένους. Στὸ μεγάλο ψυγεῖο ἀπομένει
λιγάκι βούτυρο ἀπὸ πέρυσι στὸ χαρτονένιο κουτί του. Στὴν κατάψυξη
δυὸ γυμνὲς τσίχλες κι ὁ λαμαρινένιος πετεινὸς τοῦ ἀνεμοδείχτη.

Ἀθήνα, 10.X.72

RELAPSE

If a wind comes up, if it starts to rain — hush, let me hear;
in the room next door are the scales of the maternity ward,
and dry cornstalks outside. Someone passed by — or didn't he?
You observe the cheekbones of the night — thrust forward;
you hear the crackling of the largest leaves. During intervals
you ambush the duration. Say something — but nothing contrary.
I'm not hiding it from you: I want to believe again. If you find me
    sleeping,
nudge me by the shoulder to wake me — sleep is much worse.
The train's whistle left me all alone in this house
inhabited by drowned men. In the large refrigerator you'll find
a little butter in its paper carton left over from last year. In the
    freezing compartment
are two naked thrushes and the tin weathercock.

Athens, 10/10/72

47

ΤΡΩΤΟΤΗΤΑ

Ἡ προσωπίδα ποὺ προστάτεψε τὸ πρόσωπό σου
ἔχει κολλήσει πιὰ στὸ δέρμα σου,—δὲν ξεκολλάει·
εἶναι τὸ δέρμα σου τώρα. Πληγώνεται κι αὐτὴ
ὅταν τῆς μπήγουν τὶς καρφίτσες γιὰ νὰ δοκιμάσουν
τὴν ἀντοχή της καὶ τὴν εἰλικρίνειά της. Στὸν κῆπο,
κάτω ἀπ᾽ τὴ μουσμουλιά, τὰ δυὸ παιδιὰ τοῦ λιποτάκτη
(τόνα ραχητικό, τ᾽ ἄλλο ὑδροκέφαλο) διασκεδάζουν
σπρώχνοντας μὲς στὸ στόμα τοῦ βατράχου ἕνα τσιγάρο.

Ὁ βάτραχος καπνίζει, καπνίζει. Ποτέ μου δὲν εἶδα
τίποτα πιὸ μεγάλο ἀπ᾽ τὰ μάτια τοῦ βατράχου.

Ἀθήνα, 10.Χ.72

VULNERABILITY

The mask that protected your face
has finally stuck to your skin — it won't come off;
it's your skin now. It too becomes wounded
when they stick it with pins to test
its endurance and its sincerity. In the garden
under the medlar tree, the deserter's two children
(the one rachitic, the other hydrocephalic) have fun
thrusting a cigarette into a frog's mouth.

The frog smokes and smokes. I have never before seen
anything as large as the eyes of that frog.

Athens, 10/10/72

49

ΝΥΧΤΕΡΙΝΕΣ ΠΑΡΑΣΤΑΣΕΙΣ

Ἡ γυναίκα πλαγιασμένη στὸ κρεββάτι, στραμμένη στὸν τοῖχο.
Ὁ ἄντρας λαγοκοιμᾶται στὴν καρέκλα μὲ τὰ μαῦρα γυαλιά του.
Ἡ μιά τους κόρη εἶναι στὴν κλινικὴ ἕνα μήνα τώρα. Ἡ ἄλλη
ἀνοίγει μὲ τὸ νύχι της προσεχτικὰ μιὰ τρύπα στὸ μῆλο.
Οἱ ἕντεκα νάνοι βγαίνουν ἕνας - ἕνας στὸ μπαλκόνι.
Ὁ πιὸ μικρὸς εἶναι ὁ πατέρας. Μπαίνουν πάλι μέσα
στὴ φωτισμένη κόκκινη κάμαρα. Παίρνουν τὸ στεφάνι
μὲ τὰ χάρτινα κρίνα, τὸ φοράει ὁ ἕνας στὸν ἄλλον
ἥσυχα, ταχτικά, μὲ τὴ σειρά. Μετὰ πηδοῦν ἕνας - ἕνας
ἀπέναντι, στὸ φανοστάτη· γαντζώνονται ἐκεῖ· μένουν
κανονικὰ καὶ πάλι σὰν τσαμπὶ ταριχευμένες μύγες. Ἐγὼ
δὲν ξέρω πιὰ τί νὰ κάνω. Βάζω ἕνα ποτήρι νερό. Δὲν τὸ πίνω.

Ἀθήνα, 11.X.72

NIGHTLY PERFORMANCE

The woman is lying in her bed, turned toward the wall.
Her husband with his dark glasses sits drowsing in a chair.
One of their daughters has been in a clinic a month now. The other
carefully opens a hole in an apple with her fingernail.
Five dwarfs, one by one, go out upon the balcony.
The smallest one is the father. They turn back again
into the illuminated red room, take up a wreath
of paper lilies, and one by one crown each other
quietly, orderly, each in his turn. Afterward, one by one, they jump
onto the lamp bracket opposite, hang on and stay there
at ease once more like a cluster of embalmed flies. And I
no longer know what to do. I pour water into a glass. I don't
    drink it.

Athens, 10/11/72

ΣΠΑΣΜΩΔΙΚΑ

Λαθεύω—λέει—στὸ δρόμο, λαθεύω στὸ κρεββάτι· χῶμα θέλω·
αἷμα θέλω. Μίλα· βιάσου· πράξε. Χῶμα θέλω,—λέει. Παράγγειλα
δώδεκα γλάστρες στὸν ἀγγειοπλάστη—κόκκινες γλάστρες
μὲ μιὰ τρύπα στὴ μέση. Αἷμα θέλω. Τοὺς τὄπα. Στὸ διάδρομο
πλαγιάζει τὸ σκυλὶ μὲ τὴν κόττα. Οἱ μάσκες τοῦ θεάτρου
κρέμονται ἀράδα στὸν τοῖχο. Ἐγὼ ποῦ νὰ πάω; Μεσημέρι
ἀποχρωματισμένο, χειμωνιάτικο, μαρμάρινο. Τὄδα τὸ δέντρο
ξερὸ μπροστὰ στὰ οὐρητήρια. Γύρισα πίσω. Μὲ χτύπησε
ἡ μυρωδιὰ ἀπὸ καμένο πετσί. Μπόρεσα τέλος νὰ κλάψω.
Ἔκατσα χάμου στὸ πεζοδρόμιο· ἔβγαλα τὄνα μου παπούτσι,
πῆρα ἀγκαλιὰ τὸ πόδι μου καὶ τὸ νανούρισα σὰ βρέφος. Ὅμως
ἡ κάλτσα μου εἶταν τρύπια. Φόρεσα τὸ παπούτσι μου, κ᾽ ἔφυγα.

Ἀθήνα, 11.X.72

SPASMODICALLY

I make mistakes — he says — in the street. I make mistakes in
    bed. I want earth.
I want blood. Speak, hurry, act. I want earth — he says. I've
    ordered
twelve flower pots from the potter — red pots
with holes in the middle. I want blood. I told them. In the hallway
the dog lies down with the hen. Theater masks
hang on the wall in a row. Where can I go? A noon
drained of color, wintry, like marble. I saw the tree
withered before the urinals. I turned back. An odor
of burnt flesh smote me. At last I could cry.
I sat down on the sidewalk, took off one of my shoes,
clasped my foot in my arms and rocked it like a baby. But
my sock was full of holes. I put on my shoes, and fled.

Athens, 10/11/72

ΚΟΥΡΑΣΜΕΝΗ ΕΥΧΑΡΙΣΤΙΑ

Βαθειὰ ἡσυχία κωπηλατεῖ μὲς στὰ ἴδια τὰ νερά της.
Ἡ τρελλὴ κάθησε στὴν πέτρα καὶ κοιτάει τὴ θάλασσα.
Τ' ἀγκάθια στὰ μαλλιά της εἶναι τὰ δικά μου.

'Αθήνα, 11.X.72

A WEARY THANKSGIVING

A deep tranquillity rows in its own waters.
The mad woman sat on a rock and looked at the sea.
The thorns in her eyes are my own.

Athens, 10/11/72

ΜΕΣΟΝΥΧΤΙΟΣ ΠΕΡΙΠΑΤΟΣ

Στὸ τέλος φοβήθηκε τὰ ποιήματα καὶ τὰ πολλὰ τσιγάρα·
βγῆκε μεσάνυχτα στὸ προάστιο,—ἕνας καθάριος περίπατος
ἥσυχος, πλάϊ στὰ κλειστὰ ὀπωροπωλεῖα, ἀνάμεσα
σὲ πράγματα καλὰ μὲ τὶς σωστές τους ἀόριστες διαστάσεις.
Αὐτός, συναχωμένος ἀπὸ φεγγάρι, σκουπίζει κάθε τόσο
μὲ μιὰ χαρτοπετσέτα τὴ μύτη του. Καθυστερεῖ τὸ βῆμα
ἐκεῖ μπροστὰ στὴ βαθειὰ μυρωδιὰ ἀπὸ φρέσκα τοῦβλα,
μπροστὰ στὸ ἀόρατο ἄλογο δεμένο στὸ κυπαρίσσι,
μπροστὰ στὸ λουκέτο τῆς σιταποθήκης. Ἄχ, ἔτσι—λέει—
ἀνάμεσα σὲ πράγματα ποὺ τίποτα δὲ σοῦ ἀπαιτοῦν—
κ᾽ ἕνα μικρὸ μπαλκόνι νὰ μετατοπίζεται στὸν ἀέρα
μὲ μιὰ μοναχικὴ καρέκλα. Πάνω στὴν καρέκλα
μένει παρατημένη ἀνάποδα ἡ κιθάρα τῆς νεκρῆς·
στὴ ράχη τῆς κιθάρας σπιθίζει μυστικὰ ἡ ὑγρασία—
αὐτὲς οἱ σπίθες εἶναι ποὺ ἐμποδίζουν τὸν κόσμο νὰ πεθάνει.

Ἀθήνα, 12.X.72

MIDNIGHT STROLL

In the end, afraid of the poems and the many cigarettes,
he went out at midnight to the suburb — a simple, quiet
walk along closed fruit stores, among
good things with their true, vague dimensions.
Having caught a cold from the moon, he wiped his nose
now and then with a paper napkin. He lingered
there before the pungent odor of fresh brick,
before the horse tied to a cypress tree,
before a barn's padlock. Ah, like this — he said —
among things that demand nothing of you —
and a small balcony shifting in the air
with a solitary chair. On the chair
the dead woman's guitar has been left upside down;
on the guitar's back moisture sparkles secretly —
it is sparks such as these that prevent the world from dying.

Athens, 10/12/72

ΑΤΟΛΜΙΑ

Ἐσὺ ποὺ στοχάζεσαι κι ἀμύνεσαι· ἐσὺ ποὺ λείπεις
κάνοντας τάχα πὼς μένεις κοντά μας
ἐδῶ, κάτω ἀπ' τὴ σκάλα· ἐσὺ μὲ τοὺς φίλους σου
τοὺς παλιοὺς φανοστάτες, τὰ γεφύρια—Τὸ ξέρεις ἐσύ·
τὸν ὄμορφο λοστρόμο τὸν δέσαν στὸ κατάρτι·
ἕνα μπουκάλι σόδα ἀπόμεινε στὸ τσίγκινο τραπέζι.
Ἀκοῦς, λοιπόν, τὶς φυσαλίδες; Τί ὀξυμμένη μνήμη·
τί ὀξυμμένη ἀκοή. Καὶ νὰ νιώθεις εὐχάριστα
τὸ γλύστρημα τοῦ ψαριοῦ μὲς στὸ λαρύγγι τοῦ γλάρου.

Ἀθήνα, 11.X.72

TIMIDITY

You who meditate and defend yourself; you
who are absent although you pretend to be
here, under the stair; you with your friends,
the old lamp posts. — You know:
they've tied the handsome boatswain to the mast;
a bottle of soda remains on the zinc table.
Well then, do you hear the bubbles? What a sharp memory!
What sharp hearing! And then to feel with pleasure
the fish gliding down the gull's throat.

                                    Athens, 10/11/72

ΤΟ ΤΡΙΤΟ ΠΟΙΗΜΑ

Ἀλλάζαν οἱ ἐποχές. Αὐτὸς τίποτα. Ἀπληροφόρητος πάντα.
Τὸ ἀκορντεὸν ἀκουγόταν στὸν κῆπο. Τὰ ἔντομα τῆς νύχτας
μπλέχονταν στὰ μαλλιὰ τῶν γυναικῶν. Ἐγὼ—εἶπε—
εἶδα τὴν κουκουβάγια στὸ καμπαναριό. Τὴν ἔδιωξα. Χάμω
ἔμειναν ἕνα μαῦρο κ᾽ ἕνα ἄσπρο φτερό. Ὁ ναυτικὸς
ἔσερνε μ᾽ ἕνα πέτσινο λουρὶ τὸ σκύλο του. Πέρασε
μπροστὰ στὴ φωτισμένη πόρτα τῆς ταβέρνας. Δὲν εἶταν
ἀρσενικὸ σκυλί,—γαλάζια σκύλα, ἡ θάλασσα εἶταν—εἶπε—
ἄγρια, ἑτοιμόγεννη· καὶ τὸν ἀκολουθοῦσε, ὄχι δεμένη. Τότε
φάνηκε ἡ γριὰ μ᾽ ἕνα καλάθι περασμένο στὸν ἀγκώνα της,
στάθηκε μπρὸς στὴ νεκροφόρα, σήκωσε τ᾽ ἀριστερό της χέρι
καὶ σκούπισε τὸ τσιμπλιασμένο μάτι τ᾽ ἄσπρου ἀλόγου.

Ἀθήνα, 11.X.72

THE THIRD POEM

The seasons were changing. He not at all. Uninformed always.
An accordion could be heard in the garden. The night insects
became entangled in the women's hair. I — he said —
saw the owl in the belfry. I chased it away. On the ground,
a black and white feather remained. The sailor
was dragging his dog on an enormous leash. He passed
before the illuminated door of the tavern. It was not
a male dog — it was the blue bitch, the sea — he said —
savage, ready to give birth, and it followed him, unleashed. Then
the old woman appeared with a basket slung around her elbow.
She stood before the hearse, raised her left hand
and wiped off the mucus from the horse's eye.

Athens, 10/11/72

ΤΕΛΕΤΟΥΡΓΙΚΟ

Ἀκούμπησε ἥσυχα τὸ χαρτονένιο κουτὶ στὸ τραπέζι
σὰν ἕνα κλεισμένο ἀκατοίκητο μοναστήρι. Γιὰ λίγο
μπῆκε στὸ ἄλλο δωμάτιο. Ἀκούστηκε ἡ βρύση—
μπορεῖ νὰ σαπούνισε τὰ χέρια του. Γύρισε. Ἄνοιξε
μὲ πολλὴ προσοχὴ τὸ κουτί. Ἔβαλε μέσα
τ' ἀριστερό του χέρι, μετὰ τὸ δεξί του·
ἔπιασε ἀπ' τὸν καρπὸ τ' ἀριστερό του, τὅβγαλε,
τὸ σήκωσε ψηλά, μᾶς τὅδειξε.

Ἀθήνα, 13.X.72

LITURGICAL

He placed the paper box on the table quietly
as though it were a closed, uninhabited monastery. For a while
he was gone in the other room. We could hear the faucet
   running —
perhaps he was washing his hands with soap. On returning,
he opened the box with great care and placed
his left hand within it. Then with his right hand
he grasped his left by the wrist, took it out,
raised it up high, and showed it to us.

Athens, 10/13/72

ΑΥΤΟΠΤΗΣ ΜΑΡΤΥΡΑΣ

Ἐγὼ τοὺς εἶδα—λέει—τοὺς δυὸ διαρρῆκτες πίσω ἀπ' τὶς γρίλιες
νὰ παραβιάζουν τὴν ἀπέναντι πόρτα·—δὲ φώναξα διόλου·
εἶχε φεγγάρι· φαινόνταν καθαρὰ τ' ἀντικλείδια τους
καὶ τὰ στολίδια τοῦ γύψου στὸν τοῖχο. Περίμενα πρῶτα
νὰ φωνάξουνε οἱ ἄλλοι ἀπὸ δίπλα. Κανένας δὲ φώναξε.
Ἔφυγα ἀπ' τὸ παράθυρο, κάθησα στὴν καρέκλα, ἀκούμπησα
τὸ μέτωπό μου στὸ μάρμαρο τοῦ τραπεζιοῦ, καὶ θαρρῶ
ποὺ ἀποκοιμήθηκα, πλάϊ στὸ φτωχὸ μελανωμένο χέρι
τοῦ παιδιοῦ ποὺ δὲν προβιβάστηκε. Μέσα στὸν ὕπνο μου
μ' ἔπιασε πονοκέφαλος ἀπ' τὸ φεγγάρι. Τὰ χαράματα
μοῦ χτύπησαν τὴν πόρτα. Εἶταν οἱ δυὸ διαρρῆκτες
κρατώντας δυὸ ὡραῖες ἀνθοδέσμες. Μπῆκα στὴν κουζίνα
νὰ βάλω τὰ λουλούδια στὸ νερό. Γυρίζοντας πίσω,
μ' ἕνα βάζο στὸ κάθε μου χέρι, δὲν τοὺς βρῆκα.

Ἀθήνα, 13.X.72

64

EYEWITNESS

I saw them — he said — the two burglars behind the grilles
forcing the door open opposite —. I didn't shout at all;
there was a moon, and I could see their passkeys clearly,
even the plaster ornaments on the wall. I waited
for the others next door to shout first. No one cried out.
I left the window, sat on a chair, leaned
my forehead on the marble table, and believe
I fell asleep close by the poor ink-stained hand
of the child who did not pass in school. In my sleep
I caught a headache from the moon. At daybreak
someone knocked on my door. It was the two burglars
holding two beautiful bouquets of flowers. I went into the kitchen
to put the flowers in some water. When I returned
with a vase in each hand, they had gone.

                                        Athens, 10/13/72

ΝΥΧΤΕΡΙΝΕΣ ΣΥΛΛΗΨΕΙΣ

Κουράστηκαν ἀπ' τὰ φῶτα, ἀπ' τὰ λόγια, ἀπ' τὶς πολλὲς ὁμολογίες,
ἀπ' ὅσα κρύβανε μὲ τὶς ὁμολογίες. Σώπασαν. Κοίταξαν χάμου.
Ὁ ἕνας
στάθηκε στὸ παράθυρο. Ὁ ἄλλος ξεδίπλωσε μιὰ ἐφημερίδα. Ἡ
γυναίκα
πῆγε ν' ἀδειάσει τὰ σταχτοδοχεῖα. Αἰσθάνθηκαν ἀνόρεξα ποὺ θἄ-
πρεπε
νὰ μείνουν ἀκόμα ἢ νὰ φύγουν. Βγῆκαν στὸ δρόμο. Κι ἄξαφνα,
πλάϊ, στὸ μεγάλο γήπεδο, περιφραγμένο μὲ σύρμα, σκουπισμένο,
εἶδαν τοὺς τρεῖς διπλωμάτες, μὲ ψηλὰ καπέλα, μὲ κολλαριστὰ που-
κάμισα
νὰ μαζεύουν τ' αὐγὰ ἀπ' τὸ κατάφωτο ὀρνιθοτροφεῖο. Οἱ κόττες
ὄρθιες, ξαγρυπνισμένες (λευκὲς οἱ περισσότερες) δὲ φωνάζαν,
ἁπλῶς περιεργάζονταν τ' ἀστραφτερὰ μανικετόκουμπα γνωρίζοντας
σὰν εἰδικοὶ ἐνεχυροδανειστὲς πῶς δὲν εἶταν γνήσια διαμάντια.

Ἀθήνα, 13.Χ.72

NIGHT ARRESTS

The words, the lights, the many confessions tired them,
and all they had hidden with their confessions. They fell silent,
    gazed at the floor. One man
stood by the window, the other unfolded a newspaper, the woman
    went to empty the ash trays. They felt depressed because
they might have to remain here still, or leave. They went out into
    the street. Suddenly,
in the large playing field close by, swept clean, fenced in with
    barbed wire,
they saw the three diplomats with their top hats, their starched
    shirts,
gathering eggs from the brilliantly lit chicken coop. The hens,
standing erect, wide awake (most of them white), were not
    cackling
but simply examining the glittering cufflinks with care, closely
    recognizing,
like the expert pawnbrokers they were, that these were not real
    diamonds.

Athens, 10/13/72

ΤΑΥΤΟΧΡΟΝΑ

Ἐγὼ σοῦ τόπα· δὲ σὲ γέλασα—εἶπε. Αὐτὴ ἡ στενότητα
ποὺ προχωράει ἀνάμεσα στὰ ροῦχα καὶ στὸ σῶμα, ἀνάμεσα
στὄνα καὶ στ᾽ ἄλλο σῶμα ἢ στὴ μορφὴ καὶ στὸν καθρέφτη
ἢ ἀνάμεσα στὰ χείλη καὶ στὴ λέξη. Εἶδα τὰ πανωφόρια
ἄδεια, κρεμάμενα στὸ διάδρομο, καὶ τ᾽ ἄδεια καπέλα
μὲ τὰ μικρὰ χαρτόνια καὶ τοὺς ἕτοιμους ἀριθμοὺς τυπωμένους·—
δὲ χρειαζόταν διόλου νὰ μετρήσεις. Στάσου. Κλεῖσε τὰ μάτια.
Πίσω ἀπ᾽ τὸ γύψινο ἄγαλμα εἶναι ἡ σκούπα,—τὴν εἶδα·
εἶδα καὶ τὸν ψηλὸ θαλαμηπόλο ποὖκρυβε κάτω ἀπ᾽ τὸ τραπέζι
τὸν μικρὸ κλόουν. Ὅταν περάσαν τὸν νεκρὸ ἀπ᾽ τὴν πύλη
ἀκούστηκαν πίσω τὰ κουδούνια. Ὁ μικρὸς κλόουν εἶχε μείνει
μόνος στὴν αἴθουσα τρώγοντας ἀπ᾽ τὸ δίσκο τ᾽ ἄσπρα κουφέτα.

Ἀθήνα, 14.Χ.72

68

Ἀθήνα, 14.X.72

SIMULTANEOUSLY

I told you, I haven't deceived you — he said: this tightness
that moves between the clothes and the body, between
one body and another, between the face and the mirror,
or between lips and words. I saw the empty
overcoats hanging in the hallway, and the empty hats
with their small cardboard labels, with their ready-made printed
   numbers —
it wasn't necessary to count them at all. Wait. Close your eyes.
Behind the statue is the broom — I saw it;
I also saw the tall chamberlain hiding the small clown
under the table. When they carried the dead man through the gate,
bells were heard behind him. The small clown had stayed back
in the hall, alone, eating white sugar-covered almonds from the tray.

                                        Athens, 10/14/72

69

ΜΕΤΑΘΕΣΗ

Μὲ κεῖνο τὸ ἴδιο ἀνακριβές του χαμόγελο στὰ μάτια
πλησιάζει, προθυμοποιεῖται νὰ μᾶς δείξει ἀπ' τὸ παράθυρο
τὰ δέντρα, τὴν πηγή, τὰ παρτέρια, τ' ἀγάλματα τοῦ κήπου,
ἀκόμη καὶ τὰ πέντε νοτισμένα παγκάκια. Ὡστόσο, τὴ στιγμὴ
ποὺ ὁ νεαρὸς κηπουρὸς ἐμφανίστηκε μπροστὰ στὰ χρυσάνθεμα
γυμνόστηθος, μ' ἕνα σακκούλι σπόρους, τότε, ἐκεῖνος
τράβηξε ἀμέσως τὴν κουρτίνα καὶ μᾶς ἔδειξε στὸν τοῖχο
ἕνα μεγάλο σκουριασμένο καρφὶ ἀπ' ὅπου πιὰ δὲν κρεμόταν
τὸ κάδρο μὲ τὶς δυὸ γυμνὲς γυναῖκες, τὸ φρουρὸ καὶ τὴν ἀγχόνη.

Κάλαμος, Ἀθήνα, 14.Χ.72

TRANSPOSITION

With that same imprecise smile in his eyes
he approaches, eager to show us from the window
the trees, the well, the flower-beds, the statues in the garden,
and even the five wet benches. And yet, the moment
the young gardener appeared before the chrysanthemums,
bare-chested, with a sack of seed, he then
immediately closed the curtains and showed us a large
rusted nail on the wall from which the picture no longer hung,
with its two naked women, the guard, and the gallows.

Kálamos, Athens, 10/14/72

ΤΡΟΠΟΣ ΖΩΗΣ

Ἡ κουβέρτα εἶταν πεσμένη στὸ πάτωμα. Κανένας
δὲν ἀποφάσιζε νὰ τὴ μαζέψει. Καρφιὰ καὶ πινέζες,
σκόρπιες ἐδῶ κ᾿ ἐκεῖ, μπήγονταν στὶς παντόφλες μας
ἢ καὶ στὰ πέλματά μας. Δὲ δείχναμε τίποτα.
Καθόμαστε στὸν καναπὲ ἢ σὲ μιὰ καρέκλα,
βγάζαμε τὶς πινέζες μιὰ - μιά, τὶς ἀκουμπούσαμε
στὸ μεσιανὸ τραπέζι, φανερά, μ᾿ ἕνα ὕφος θύματος
καὶ νικητῆ ταυτόχρονα, ἴσως ἀπ᾿ τὸ ὅτι
δὲν εἴχαμε φωνάξει στὴν κρίσιμη στιγμή. Ἔτσι
μαζέψαμε ἀπ᾿ τὸ πάτωμα καρφιὰ καὶ πινέζες.
Τὴν κουβέρτα τὴν ἀφήσαμε ἐκεῖ.

Κάλαμος, 15.X.72

WAY OF LIFE

The blanket had fallen to the floor. No one
could decide to pick it up. Nails and thumbtacks,
scattered here and there, lodged in our slippers
or even in the soles of our feet. We didn't reveal a thing.
We sat on a couch or a chair,
pulled out the thumbtacks one by one, placed them
on the middle table openly, with the air of a victim
and victor both, perhaps because we had
made no sound at the critical moment. And so
we picked up the nails and the thumbtacks from the floor.
We left the blanket where it had fallen.

Kálamos, 10/15/72

ΑΒΕΒΑΙΗ ΘΕΡΑΠΕΙΑ

Τὸ παιδὶ μὲ τὴν ἀκέφαλη κούκλα· ἡ γυναίκα μὲ τὴ βελόνα·
ὁ ἄντρας μὲ τὸ ξύλινο ζωγραφισμένο ψάρι· ἡ ἄλλη γυναίκα
λιγνή, μαραγκιασμένη, μὲ τὰ δυὸ μαδημένα φτερά της
κρυμμένα μὲς στὴ φούστα της, κρατημένα ἀπ᾽ τὴ ζώνη,
νὰ δείχνει κάπως πιὸ παχειά· ὁ δεύτερος ἄντρας
μὲ δυὸ ἀσπιρίνες στὴν παλάμη του μπροστὰ στὸ παράθυρο
κοιτάει τὸν ταχυδρομικὸ διανομέα·—πέρασε· δὲ στάθηκε. Ὅλοι,
μόνος καθένας μέσα στὴ δική του ἀναμονή, ψάχνοντας
τὴ λέξη ποὺ θἄλεγαν. Μόνον ἐγὼ τοὺς εἶδα καὶ τοὺς τὄπα
μὲ σιγανὴ πανένια φωνή, κρυμμένος πίσω ἀπ᾽ τὴν κουρτίνα,
γυμνὸς ἐγώ, κρατώντας τὸ κομμένο κεφάλι τῆς κούκλας.

Κάλαμος, 15.Χ.72

74

DOUBTFUL THERAPY

The child with the headless doll, the woman with the needle,
the man with the painted wooden fish; the other woman,
lean, withered, with her two moulted wings
hidden in her skirt and held by her belt
that she might seem fatter; the second man
before the window, with two aspirins in his hand,
watching the mailman, who did not stop but passed on. Each one
alone, each with his own expectations, searching
for a word to say. Only I saw them and told them
with a quiet homespun voice, hiding behind the curtain,
I, naked, holding the severed head of the doll.

Kálamos, 10/15/72

ΠΡΑΓΜΑΤΙΚΑ ΧΕΡΙΑ

Αὐτὸς ποὺ χάθηκε ἀνεξήγητα ἕνα ἀπόγευμα (ἴσως
καὶ νὰ τὸν πῆραν) εἶχε ἀφήσει στὸ τραπέζι τῆς κουζίνας
τὰ μάλλινα γάντια του σὰ δυὸ κομμένα χέρια
ἀναίμακτα, ἀδιαμαρτύρητα, γαλήνια, ἢ μᾶλλον
σὰν τὰ ἴδια του τὰ χέρια, λίγο πρησμένα, γεμισμένα
μὲ τὸ χλιαρὸν ἀέρα μιᾶς πανάρχαιης ὑπομονῆς. Ἐκεῖ,
ἀνάμεσα στὰ χαλαρά, μάλλινα δάχτυλα,
βάζουμε πότε - πότε μιὰ φέτα ψωμί, ἕνα λουλούδι
ἢ τὸ ποτήρι τοῦ κρασιοῦ μας, ξέροντας καθησυχαστικὰ
ὅτι στὰ γάντια τουλάχιστον δὲν μπαίνουν χειροπέδες.

Κάλαμος, 15.Χ.72

REAL HANDS

He who disappeared inexplicably one afternoon (perhaps
they came and took him) had left on the kitchen table
his woolen mittens like two severed hands,
bloodless, uncomplaining, serene, or rather
exactly like his own hands, a bit swollen, filled
with the tepid air of a very ancient endurance. There,
between the slack woolen fingers
we would place from time to time a slice of bread, a flower,
or our own wineglass, in the knowledge
that gloves, at least, can't be handcuffed.

Kálamos, 10/15/72

ΑΤΑΦΟΙ

Νεκροὶ μὲς σὲ μεγάλα ψυγεῖα, περιμένοντας
ἀπελπισμένοι ἢ προνοητικοὶ (ὄχι ἐκεῖνοι—ἐμεῖς)
μπροστὰ σὲ κάτασπρα πανύψηλα τοιχώματα
κ' ἡ οὐρὰ τοῦ κόκκινου ψαριοῦ πιασμένη στὴν πόρτα.

Κάλαμος, 15.Χ.72

UNBURIED

The dead in large refrigerators, waiting
in desperation or in premonition (not they — but we)
before pure white towering masonry
and the tail of the red fish caught in the door.

Kálamos, 10/15/72

ΕΣΠΕΡΙΝΟΣ

Περίλυπο ἀπόγευμα, μενεξεδί, βυσσινί, καρφωμένο
στὶς πόρτες τοῦ παλιοῦ προαστίου, στοὺς γδαρμένους τοίχους
καὶ στὴ μεγάλη πινακίδα τοῦ γκαράζ. Τίποτα δὲν ἀκολουθεῖ
τὸ πέρασμα τῆς ἀστυνομικῆς μοτοσυκλέτας. Ἐγὼ—εἶπε—
κ᾽ ἔδειξε πρὸς τ᾽ ἀντίθετο μέρος, κάτω ἀπ᾽ τὰ φῶτα τῆς Λέσχης
ποὺ ἀνάψαν μονομιᾶς:—ὁ νεαρὸς θηριοδαμαστὴς
μὲ χρυσὰ πέδιλα, μ᾽ ἕνα μακρὺ μαστίγιο τυλιγμένο
τριγύρω στὸ λαιμό του, προχωρεῖ ἀπὸ πόρτα σὲ πόρτα
ὣς τὰ μεγάλα κλουβιά· χώνει τὸ χέρι του μὲς στὸ λαρύγγι
τοῦ λιονταριοῦ, σὰ νὰ φράζει μιὰ τρύπα στὸ δικό του σῶμα,
ἐνῶ οἱ ἐννέα χορεύτριες στὰ ὁλόλευκα παρατηροῦν
ἀσάλευτες, παραταγμένες κατὰ μῆκος τοῦ διαδρόμου.

Ἀθήνα, 16.X.72

VESPERS

A gloomy afternoon, violet, maroon, nailed
on the doors of the old suburb, on the chafed walls
and the garage's large sign. Nothing follows
after the police motorcycle has passed. I — he said —
and pointed to the opposite side under the lights of the Clubhouse
which had flared up suddenly — to the young animal trainer
with golden sandals, and who with a long whip wrapped around
his neck, advances from door to door
until he reaches the large cages, then thrusts his hands
into the lion's throat, as though he were plugging up a hole in his
    own body,
while the nine dancers clad all in white look on,
motionless, arranged along the length of the corridor.

Athens, 10/16/72

ΜΙΚΡΗ ΣΟΝΑΤΑ

Ἄξαφνα τὸ κεφάλι τοῦ πιανίστα ἀπόγειρε κ' ἔμεινε
πάνω στὰ πλῆκτρα, κάπως λοξά. Ὁ βιολιστὴς
συνέχισε μόνος του, χωρὶς νὰ κοιτάει
τοὺς θαμῶνες ἢ τὰ γκαρσόνια. Οἱ νικελένιοι δίσκοι
λάμπαν ἀσάλευτοι στὸν ἀέρα καθρεφτίζοντας
μιὰ μεγάλη σειρὰ μαῦρα ἀναλόγια ὣς μέσα
στὴ γυναικεία τουαλέτα ὅπου χτενίζονταν
οἱ τρεῖς ὡραῖες κυρίες μὲ κόκκινες τσατσάρες.
Ἡ συγχορδία τῆς διακοπῆς ἔσβηνε στὰ μαλλιά τους.

Ἀθήνα, 16.Χ.72

SMALL SONATA

Suddenly the head of the pianist slumped and leaned
on the piano keys, somewhat ashen. The violinists
continued alone, without looking
at the customers or the waiters. The nickel trays
glittered motionless in the air, reflecting
a long series of black music stands far into
the women's toilet where three beautiful ladies
were arranging their hair with red combs.
The chord of the intermission subsided in their hair.

Athens, 10/16/72

ΤΟ ΠΟΙΗΜΑ ΚΙ Ο ΠΟΙΗΤΗΣ

Ἐκεῖνο τὸ ποίημα τ' ἄκουσες; Εἶδες τὴ γλώσσα τῆς τίγρης
μὲς στὸ κλουβί;—κόκκινη γλώσσα, δηλητηριώδης, ἀνάμεσα
στὰ αἰχμηρὰ κατάλευκα δόντια της. Ἡ μέρα ἁπλωνόταν
στὰ πέτρινα σκαλιὰ τῆς ἐκκλησίας. Οἱ τρεῖς τυφλοὶ
μὲ τὰ καπέλα τους στὰ γόνατά τους, ξεχασμένοι,
ἀνάψαν τσιγάρο καὶ τόσβησαν ἀμέσως. Ἀργότερα
πέρασε ὁ ἀρκουδιάρης μὲ τὸ ντέφι του βαμμένο στὸ λιόγερμα
κόκκινο, κατακόκκινο σὰν αἷμα. Τὰ παιδιὰ δὲ μαζεύτηκαν.

Εἶδες τὴ γλώσσα τῆς τίγρης, τὸ βράδι, νὰ γλείφει τὸ βρέφος της
μὲς στὸ ἴδιο κλουβί, φωτισμένο ἀπ' τ' ἀπέναντι φῶτα
τῶν δυὸ ἐστιατορίων καὶ τοῦ μεγάλου κλειστοῦ ἀνθοπωλείου;
Ἐγὼ τοὺς τόπα ἀπὸ πρίν,—δὲ γελάστηκα μήτε τοὺς γέλασα.

Ἀθήνα, 16.Χ.72

THE POEM AND THE POET

That poem — did you hear it? Did you see the tigress's tongue
in the cage — a red tongue, venomous, between
her pointed gleaming teeth? The day spread
on the stone steps of the church. The three blind men
with their hats on their knees, forgotten,
lit their cigarettes and put them out immediately. Later
the bear trainer passed by with his tambourine painted red
in the sunset, as red as blood. The children never gathered.

Did you see the tigress's tongue in the evening licking her cub
in the same cage, lit up by the lights opposite
coming from the two restaurants and the large closed flower shop?
I told them beforehand — I was not deceived, nor had I
    deceived them.

Athens, 10/16/72

85

ΣΤΑΔΙΑ ΑΓΝΟΙΑΣ

Ἐκεῖνο ποὺ ὀνειρεύτηκε σὰν στήριγμα, μέρα τὴ μέρα τοῦ ἀφαιροῦσε
ὅλα του τὰ στηρίγματα. Παρατηροῦσε πίσω ἀπ᾽ τὰ τζάμια
νὰ διακρίνει ὅ,τι εἶχε ἐγκαταλείψει—τὴν καρέκλα τοῦ κήπου,
τὸν παλιό, μαυρισμένο καπνοδόχο, αὐτὸν ποὺ κάποτε
εἶχε ὀνομάσει ἀκέφαλο ἄγαλμα, κ᾽ εἶχαν κ᾽ οἱ δυὸ συμφωνήσει
μὲ τὴν ἁπλὴ συμφωνία δυὸ λυπημένων ξένων
χωρὶς ἀμοιβαῖες ἀξιώσεις κι ἀνταγωνισμούς. Λίγο ἀργότερα, ὡστόσο,
καθὼς ἀνέβαινε τὴ σκάλα μεταμφιεσμένος σὲ τυφλό,
ὁ ἀληθινὸς τυφλός, κρυμμένος μὲς στὸ κοίλωμα τοῦ τοίχου,
τοῦ ἅρπαξε ἄξαφνα τὰ μαῦρα γυαλιά του, κ᾽ ἐκεῖνος
ὑποχρεώθηκε νὰ κλείσει (ἴσως γιὰ πάντα) τὰ μάτια
μὴ καὶ προδώσει ἢ ἀνασκευάσει τὴν προηγούμενη ζωή του
ἂν καὶ δὲν ἤξερε καθόλου τί εἶταν ἡ ζωή του καὶ γενικὰ ἡ ζωή.

Ἀθήνα, 17.X.72

86

STAGES OF IGNORANCE

What he dreamt of as a support had day by day removed
all his supports. Behind the windowpane he watched
to distinguish all he had abandoned — the garden chair,
the old sooty chimney-stack he had once
called a headless statute, and they had both agreed
with that simple agreement between two saddened strangers
who had no mutual pretensions or rivalries. A little later,
    nevertheless,
as he was climbing the stairs disguised as a blind man,
the real blind man, hidden in a niche within the wall,
suddenly snatched away his dark glasses, and he was then
compelled to close his eyes (perhaps forever)
lest he betray or refute his previous life,
even though he didn't at all know what his life was, or even
    life in general.

Athens, 10/17/72

ΣΥΝΗΘΗΣ ΑΙΦΝΙΔΙΑΣΜΟΣ

Φόρεσα λαστιχένια παπούτσια, πῆρα ἀπὸ πίσω τὸν κωφάλαλο·
στὴ δεύτερη στάση, γύρισε, μὲ κοίταξε. «Μοῦ δίνεις—εἶπε—
τὰ λαστιχένια παπούτσια σου;». Τἄβγαλα. Τοῦ τἄδωσα. Ἔφυγα.
Μὲ πῆρε ἀπὸ πίσω. Μπῆκα στὸ τραῖνο. Εἶχε θέση. Κάθησα.
Ἀπέναντί μου αὐτός. Ἀνάψαμε τσιγάρο. Κοιτούσαμε
ἔξω ἀπ' τὰ τζάμια τὰ δέντρα, γυμνά, μὲ τοὺς βρεγμένους σπάγγους
τῶν παιδικῶν χαρταητῶν, μὲ τὰ παλιὰ κατσαρόλια τοῦ συσσίτιου
τῶν ἐξορίστων. Καπνίζαμε. Κάναμε πὼς δὲ γνωριζόμαστε—
ἐγὼ ξυπόλυτος, κι αὐτὸς μὲ τὰ παπούτσια μου, καθόλου ὑπερόπτης.

Ἀθήνα, 18.X.72

HABITUAL SURPRISE

I put on my rubber shoes and followed the deaf-mute.
At the second station, he turned and looked at me. "Will you
    give me," he said,
"your rubber shoes?" I took them off, gave them to him, and left.
He followed me. I got on the train, found a seat, sat down.
He sat down opposite me. We both lit a cigarette. We both looked
out of the window at barren trees hung with the wet strings
of children's kites, with the old pots and pans of the political
    prisoners' mess-hall.
We smoked, pretending not to know one another —
I barefooted, and he with my shoes, not arrogant at all.

Athens, 10/18/72

ΣΧΕΔΙΑΣΜΑ ΕΦΙΑΛΤΗ

«Κρού, γκρόου», «κρού γκρόου», ἐπαναλάβαινε πάλι καὶ πάλι·
«κρού, γκρόου», μπροστὰ στὸν καθρέφτη της, πεισμένη ἡ ἴδια
γιὰ τὴν ἀκρίβεια τοῦ ἤχου·—αὐτὴ ἡ νεότερη γριὰ τοῦ κόσμου
αὐτὴ μὲ τὰ σαρκώδη χείλη· αὐτὴ ποὺ τριβόταν στοὺς ἄντρες
χορεύοντας κάτω ἀπ' τὰ γαλάζια φῶτα. Κ' ἡ ἀφίσα τοῦ τοίχου
νὰ δείχνει τὴν κουλὴ χοντρὴ γυναίκα μὲ τὰ δώδεκα πόδια,
μὲ τὰ ἕξη αἰδοῖα, κρατώντας ἀνάμεσα στὰ δόντια της
τὸ μεγάλο τσιγγέλι τοῦ χασάπη ἀπ' ὅπου κρεμόταν
γδαρμένη, κατακόκκινη, ἡ εὐνοούμενη ἀγελάδα τοῦ Ἀπόλλωνα.

Ἀθήνα, 18.Χ.72

OUTLINE OF A NIGHTMARE

"Krou, grou, krou grou," she repeats over and over again;
"krou, grou," before her mirror, utterly convinced
by the accuracy of the sound — this youngest crone in the world,
she with the fleshy lips, she who rubbed up against men
as she danced under blue lights. And the billboard on the wall
showed the armless stout woman with twelve feet,
with six vaginas, holding between her teeth
a large butcher's hook from which hung,
skinned and blood-red, Apollo's favorite cow.

Athens, 10/18/72

ΤΟ ΝΟΗΜΑ ΤΗΣ ΤΕΧΝΗΣ

Στὸν Hubert Juin

Ὧρες κοιτοῦσε τὸ κομμένο χέρι τοῦ ἀγάλματος—μονάχα ἕνα χέρι
σταματημένο σὲ μιὰν ἥσυχη χειρονομία ἀνασυγκρότησης
ὁλόκληρου τοῦ σώματός του. Ἔτσι, ἴσως νἄχε μάθει
τὸ βαθὺ μυστικὸ ποὺ δὲ θἄπρεπε κι αὐτὸς νὰ τὸ πεῖ. Κι ἄλλωστε
ποιὸς θὰ μποροῦσε, καὶ πῶς, νὰ τὸ πεῖ; Ἡ ποίηση—εἶπε—
ἀρχίζει πάντοτε πρὶν ἀπ' τὶς λέξεις ἢ μετὰ τὶς λέξεις. Τότε
εἴδαμε τὸ πουλὶ ποὺ βγῆκε ἀπ' τὸ κομμένο χέρι κ' ἔκατσε στὸ ψωμί.

Ἀθήνα, 18.X.72

THE MEANING OF ART

To Hubert Juin

For hours he gazed at the statue's severed hand — only one
      hand
stopped in a quiet gesture toward the reconstruction
of its entire body. Perhaps in this way he had learned
the deep secret not even he must reveal. And besides,
who would be able to reveal it, and how? Poetry — he said —
always begins before the words or after the words. It was then
we saw the bird as it emerged out of the severed hand and sat
      on a loaf of bread.

Athens, 10/18/72

ΑΝΤΙΣΤΑΣΗ ΣΤΟ ΑΟΡΙΣΤΟ

Ἡ ἄρρωστη γυναίκα μπροστὰ στὸ παράθυρο, ξαγρυπνισμένη
ἀπὸ τὸ γαύγισμα τοῦ φεγγαριοῦ. Ἡ ἄλλη, στ' ἄλλο δωμάτιο,
δοκίμαζε στ' ἀριστερό της χέρι τὰ κλεμμένα γάντια
τῶν παλιῶν ἐραστῶν της. Ἡ τρίτη γυναίκα στὴν κουζίνα
ἔπλενε τὰ ποτήρια. Οἱ δυὸ ἄντρες κοιμόνταν
ὁ ἕνας στὸν καναπέ, ὁ ἄλλος στὴν πολυθρόνα. Ἡ κουρτίνα
σάλεψε μόνη της ἀδιόρατα, δίστασε, στάθηκε
κι ἀμέσως σωριάστηκε καταμεσὶς τῆς κάμαρας, κρύβοντας
ἐκεῖνο τὸ ἀντικείμενο ἢ τὸ ζῶο ἢ τὸ πουλὶ ποὺ κανένας
δὲν εἶχε προφτάσει νὰ δεῖ. Σωπάστε,—φώναξε ὁ τρίτος—σωπάστε,
(ἂν καὶ κανεὶς δὲ μιλοῦσε), σωπάστε ἐπιτέλους—
θέλω ν' ἀκούσω μιὰ λέξη ὥς τὸ τέλος, ν' ἀκούσω
αὐτὸν ποὺ λέει «πονάω» καὶ δείχνει τ' ὁρισμένο μέρος
τὸ δόντι, τὴν καρδιά, τὸ στομάχι, τὴ φτέρνα ἢ τὸ πέος.

                                                    Ἀθήνα, 18.X.72

RESISTANCE TO THE INDEFINITE

The sick woman before the window, sleepless
from the barking of the moon. The other woman, in the other room,
trying out, on her left hand, the gloves she had stolen
from her old lovers. The third woman in the kitchen
washing dishes. The two men sleeping,
one on the couch, the other on the armchair. The curtain
stirred by itself imperceptibly, hesitated, stopped,
and immediately collapsed in the middle of the room, hiding
that object or that animal or that bird which no one
was in time to see. Be quiet — the third man shouted — be quiet
(although no one had spoken), be quiet, for God's sake —
I want to hear, to hear one word to the end, to hear
that man who says "I'm in pain" and points to a specific place,
to a tooth, heart, stomach, heel, or penis.

Athens, 10/18/72

ΤΟ ΓΔΥΣΙΜΟ ΤΟΥ ΚΡΕΜΑΣΜΕΝΟΥ

Τὸν εἶδα—λέει—μὲ τὰ μάτια μου· κρεμόταν ὁλόκληρος
ἀπ' τὸ χαμόγελό του ἕνα μέτρο ψηλὰ σὰν ἀπὸ γάντζο
κρατημένον στὰ δόντια του. Δὲν ἔπαιζε τὰ βλέφαρα. Πλησίασα·
τοῦ ξέλυσα τὴ ζώνη, τοὔβγαλα τὸ βρακί, τὸ σώβρακο. Τὸν κοίταξα.
Μισόκλεισε τὄνα του μάτι κατανεύοντας. ("Ω, αὐτὸ περίμενε—
μὲ πόση ἀπελπισμένη εὐγένεια, πόση πανουργία. Δὲν τολμοῦσε
ν' ἀναλάβει ἀπὸ μόνος τὴν εὐθύνη). Στὶς τσέπες του
σακκάκι, παντελόνι, τίποτα δὲ βρῆκα, μόνον
πέντε σπασμένες ὀδοντογλυφίδες. Τὸν ἄφησα κ' ἔφυγα. Τὸ βράδι
ποὺ ξαναπέρασα ἀπὸ περιέργεια δὲν εἶταν ἐκεῖ.

Ἀθήνα, 19.Χ.72

THE UNDRESSING OF THE HANGED MAN

I saw him — he said — with my own eyes; he was hanging one
    meter high
entirely from his smile, as though from a hook
held in his teeth. His eyelids were not blinking. I approached,
loosened his belt, took off his trousers, his shorts, and looked at him.
He half-closed one of his eyes, nodding. (Oh, this is what he had
    been waiting for,
with how much despairing civility, how much cunning. He had
    never dared
assume the responsibility himself.) In the pockets
of his coat and trousers I found nothing, only
five broken toothpicks. I left him, and went away. In the evening,
when I passed by again out of curiosity, he was not there.

Athens, 10/19/72

ΟΡΙΑ

Πῶς τοὺς ἀντέχουμε—ἔλεγε—τόσους θανάτους, τὸ δικό μας θάνατο;
   Μὲς στὴ ντουλάπα
κρέμονται ἀκόμη ροῦχα καὶ ροῦχα σὲ ἄσπρες νάϋλον σακκοῦλες
δεμένες ἐπάνω μὲ σπάγγους, μὲ κόκκινες ἢ κίτρινες ταινίες
ἀπὸ δέματα ζαχαροπλαστείων. Ἡ ναφθαλίνη πιὰ δὲ μυρίζει.
   Ποιὸς τάχα
νὰ τὰ φοροῦσε; σὲ ποιὸ μέρος; σὲ ποιὸ χρόνο; Πιθανὸν
νἆναι καὶ τὰ δικά μας παλιωμένα, ἀφόρετα, ξεθωριασμένα. Πιὸ κάτω
οἱ πέτσινες ζῶνες καὶ τὰ γάντια κ' οἱ δυὸ χειμωνιάτικες ὀμπρέλες,
μιὰ μαβιὰ καὶ μιὰ μαύρη. Ὅμως αὐτὲς τὶς δώσαμε μιὰ νύχτα κα-
   ταιγίδας
στὸ θυρωρὸ καὶ στὴ γυναίκα του νὰ συνοδέψουν στὸ σταθμὸ τοῦ
   τραίνου
τὴν ξένη κυρία μὲ τὴν κόκκινη περούκα καὶ τὰ δυὸ μουσκεμένα
   σκυλιά της
ποὺ τρέμαν σύγκορμα κρατώντας στὰ δόντια τους ἀπὸ μιὰ μαύρη
   βαλίτσα.

                                                    Ἀθήνα, 19.Χ.72

LIMITS

How can we endure — he said — so many deaths, our own death?
    In the wardrobe
garment after garment still hang in white nylon bags
tied at the top with string, with red or yellow ribbons
from pastry-shop packages. The moth-balls smell no longer
    lingers. Who
can have worn them? In what place? In what year? They are
    probably
ours grown old, never worn, faded. A bit below are
leather belts and gloves and two winter umbrellas,
one dark blue and one black. But these we gave one stormy night
to the janitor and his wife so they could escort to the train station
the foreign lady with her red wig and her two drenched dogs
trembling bodily as each held between its teeth a black suitcase.

                                                    Athens, 10/19/72

ΣΥΝΟΙΚΙΑ «ΘΥΜΑΡΑΚΙΑ», 1939

Ἡ μιὰ γυναίκα στὸ παράθυρο, καμπούρα. «Περσεφόνη», φωνάζει.
Ἡ ἄλλη στὴν αὐλὴ μὲ τὰ λάχανα, σὲ μιὰ καρέκλα. Στὶς τσέπες της
φυλάει ἀκόμη τὰ εἰσιτήρια τοῦ κυριακάτικου σινεμά. Οἱ δυὸ ξένοι
κρατᾶνε τέσσερα ἄδεια, ὡραῖα, πολύχρωμα κλουβιά. Τὰ παζαρεύουν
μὲ τὶς πιὸ κάτω γυναῖκες·—δὲν ξέρουν τὴ γλώσσα μας. Κουνᾶνε
τὰ δάχτυλά τους, δείχνουν ἀριθμούς. Ὁ μουγγὸς πλησιάζει,
ἀγοράζει τὰ δυό. Μ' ἕνα κλουβὶ σὲ κάθε χέρι, ἀνεβαίνει
τὴν πέτρινη σκάλα τοῦ Σταθμοῦ· γυρνάει, μᾶς κοιτάει ἀπὸ πάνω,
σαλεύει τὰ κλουβιά του σὰ νᾶναι νὰ φωνάξει ἢ νὰ πετάξει—
δὲ φώναξε ὅμως, οὔτε πέταξε· κελάηδησε μόνον—αὐτὸ τ' ἀκούσαμε
    ὅλοι—
ἐκτὸς κι ἂν εἶταν μέσα στὰ κλουβιὰ τὰ πουλιὰ ποὺ δὲν εἶχε ἀγοράσει.

                                           Ἀθήνα, 19.X.72

100

THE DISTRICT "THIMARAKIS," 1939

One woman by the window, a hunchback. "Persephone," she shouts.
The other with vegetables in the courtyard, on a chair. In her pockets
she still keeps the ticket stubs from a Sunday movie. Two strangers
hold four empty, beautiful, multicolored cages. They bargain for them
with two women a little further down, not knowing our language.
   They shake
their fingers, point out numbers. The mute approaches,
buys two of the cages. With one in either hand, he ascends
the Station's stone steps, turns, looks at us from above,
swings them as though he were about to shout or fly —
but he doesn't shout, nor does he fly. He only sings — this we
   all heard —
unless in the cage there were birds he had not bought.

Athens, 10/19/72

ΜΕΤΑ ΤΗΝ ΕΞΟΦΛΗΣΗ ΤΩΝ ΧΡΕΩΝ

Δὲν εἶχε τί νὰ πεῖ. Τάϊσε τοὺς κουλούς. Ἔγραψε τὶς παραγγελιές του
στ᾽ ἄδειο πακέτο τῶν τσιγάρων του· τ᾽ ἄφησε στὸ τραπέζι
γιὰ τοὺς πέντε κωφάλαλους τοῦ ἄλλου δωματίου. Τὸ ξύλινο πόδι
τὸ ἀκούμπησε ὄρθιο στὴ γωνιὰ τοῦ λουτροῦ. Βγῆκε στὸ πλαϊνὸ
χωράφι,
πῆγε στὸ σπίτι τοῦ σκύλου, τοῦ ἄλλαξε νερό,—δὲν τὸν χάϊδεψε. Τὸ
βράδι
γύρισε πιὸ νωρὶς ἀπὸ ἄλλοτε. Οἱ τροχονόμοι φεῦγαν ἀπ᾽ τοὺς
δρόμους
μ᾽ αὐτὴ τὴν αἴσθηση μιᾶς ἄγνωστης πάντα ὑγρασίας στ᾽ ἄσπρο περι-
βραχιόνιό τους
καὶ στ᾽ ἄσπρα τους γάντια. Ποιὰ τάχα τιμωρία νὰ ἑτοίμαζε
μέσα στὴν εὐσπλαχνία του, ποιὰν ἀνταπόδοση; Ὅταν βγῆκε τὸ
φεγγάρι
ἔλαμψε νοτισμένο τὸ παγκάκι τῆς πλατείας, ὁλότελα μόνο
σὰ νάταν νὰ καθήσει ἐκεῖ, νὰ βγάλει τὰ παπούτσια του ὁ θεός.

                                        Ἀθήνα, 20.X.72

102

AFTER A SETTLEMENT OF DEBTS

He had nothing to say. He fed the mutes, wrote on his empty
     cigarette box
what he wanted ordered, and left it on the table
for the five deaf-mutes in the other room. He leaned the wooden leg
upright in a corner of the bathroom, then went out to the field
     next door,
to the dog house, and changed the water there — but he didn't
     pat the dog. In the evening,
he returned earlier than usual. Traffic cops were leaving the streets
with a sense of a dampness forever unknown on their white bands
and their white gloves. What possible punishment is he preparing
in his compassion, what retaliation? When the moon came out,
the small bench in the town square shone with moisture, utterly
     alone,
as though God was going to sit there and take off His shoes.

Athens, 10/20/72

ΑΛΛΟΥ

Ἡ αἴθουσα λαμπερή, σφουγγαρισμένη ὥς πέρα ἀπ᾽ τὰ παράθυρά της,
ὣς τὸ τεράστιο φεγγάρι καὶ τὴ μάντρα τοῦ νεκροταφείου. Οἱ
πολυθρόνες
ξύλινες, σκαλιστές, βαλμένες στὴ σειρά, τοῖχο-τοῖχο.
Πάνω σὲ κάθε πολυθρόνα ἕνα ζευγάρι μαῦρα γάντια. Στὸν
πολυέλαιο
μεγάλες μύγες μὲ πράσινα φωσφορίζοντα μάτια. Κανένας
δὲ μπῆκε, δὲ βγῆκε. Νεκρὴ καθαρότητα, ἀκρίβεια, τάξη,
πρὶν καὶ μετὰ τὴν ὁρισμένη ἀναμονή. Τὸ πάτωμα πλυμένο
ἀπ᾽ τὰ αἵματα καὶ τὰ μαλλιά, ποὖχαν κουρέψει τὸ μικρὸ βασιλέα.
Κάποιος
θἄχε φωνάξει ἢ θὰ φωνάξει ἀπὸ στιγμὴ σὲ στιγμὴ «Κρανιούου,
Κρανιοῦ».
Κλεῖσε τ᾽ αὐτιά σου—«Κρανιούου»—προτιμότερη ἡ μετάθεση ἐκείνη
ἀπ᾽ τὸ ν᾽ ἀφήσεις νὰ σὲ κυβερνήσει ὁ ἀπόλυτος λόγος ποὺ δὲν εἶπες.

Ἀθήνα, 21.Χ.72

ELSEWHERE

The hall glittered, scrubbed through and through from its windows
to the enormous moon and the cemetery wall. The armchairs
were wooden, carved, arranged in a row against the wall.
On each armchair, a pair of black gloves; only on the third
to the right, a pair completely white. No one
came in or out. A lifeless cleanliness, precision, orderliness
before and after the appointed expectation. The floor washed clean
of the blood and hair they had shorn from the small king. Someone
must have shouted, or was about to shout from moment to
    moment, "Skull, Skull!"
Stop up your ears — "Skull!" — far better that transference
than permitting yourself to be governed by the absolute word
    you never uttered.

                                              Athens, 10/21/72

105

ΓΡΗΓΟΡΗ ΣΚΟΥΡΙΑ

Τί ὄμορφα ποὖχες κοιμηθεῖ πάνω στὰ δέντρα. Ὅταν γύρισες πίσω
βρῆκες τὰ κάγκελα τοῦ κήπου σκουριασμένα κιόλας ἀπ' τ' ἁλάτι.
Ἡ κόκκινη νάϋλον κουλούρα γιὰ τὸ κολύμπι τῶν παιδιῶν
κρεμόταν ξεφούσκωτη στὴν πρόκα τῆς μάντρας. Τίποτα—εἶπε.
Ἄγγιξε τὸ ψαθὶ τῆς ὑπαίθριας καρέκλας. Δὲν κάθησε.
Οἱ ταξιδιῶτες περάσαν,—τὸ καπέλο τους κατεβασμένο στὰ φρύδια.
Μιὰ κίνηση—ὄχι μετακίνηση, μ' ἕνα μικρὸ καθρέφτη στὴν τσάντα,
μὲ μιὰ τσατσάρα στὴν τσέπη τους. Ἀπέναντι, στὸ βρεγμένο χωράφι,
οἱ τρεῖς μεθυσμένοι ἁμαξάδες γεμίζουν μὲ ξερὸ χορτάρι
τὸ μακρὺ νυφικὸ τῆς πεθαμένης. Γιὰ κεφάλι τοῦ βάλαν
κεῖνο τὸ ψόφιο κοράκι ποὺ ξέβρασε χθὲς βράδι ἡ φουρτούνα.

Κάλαμος, 21.Χ.72

RAPID CORROSION

How beautifully you had slept in the trees. When you returned
you found the garden railing already corroded by the brine.
The red plastic inner tube the children used in swimming
was hanging deflated on a nail of the courtyard wall. Nothing —
    he said.
He touched the straw matting of the outdoor chair, but didn't sit
    down.
Travelers passed by, their hats drawn down to their eyebrows.
A movement — not a change of position — with a small mirror in
    their wallets,
A comb in their pockets. Opposite, in the wet field,
three drunken coachmen fill with dry grass
the dead woman's long wedding gown. For a head they place on it
a dead crow washed up by the storm last night.

Kálamos, 10/21/72

ΜΕ ΤΗΝ ΑΚΡΗ ΤΟΥ ΜΑΤΙΟΥ

Ἔνοχοι ὄχι· ἐνοχοποιημένοι. Ἡ ἀγριαπιδιὰ μπροστὰ στὸ παράθυρο.
Ἔρημο τὸ κουτσὸ σκυλὶ γυρνώντας ἔξω ἀπ' τὸ κλειστὸ θερινὸ σπίτι.
Πόσο εἶχες μελετήσει τὴ σιωπὴ πλάϊ στοὺς νεκροὺς πυροσβέστες
μὲ τὰ κράνη τους πεσμένα στὰ κίτρινα χόρτα. Εἶχες κρατήσει
καθαρὰ τὰ σημάδια στὸ λαστιχένιο σωλήνα τοῦ κήπου. Ὁ τυφλὸς
χτύπησε τὸ ραβδί του στὰ χαλίκια, μετὰ στὸ νερό. Κατάλαβε. Γύρι-
σε πίσω. Τότε
ἔκανες νὰ τὸν ὁδηγήσεις στ' ἀντικρινὸ πεζοδρόμιο. Ἐκεῖνος
ἀρνήθηκε ἥσυχα. Σοῦ χαμογέλασε. Ἔβγαλε τὸ καπέλο του
καὶ σοῦδωσε τὰ τρία τραπουλόχαρτα πούχες κρύψει ἐκεῖ μέσα.
Ὅμως ἐσὺ δὲν ἤξερες τίποτα. Ἐσύ 'σουν χειρουργός.

Κάλαμος, 22.Χ.72

108

WITH THE CORNER OF THE EYE

Guilty, no; implicated. The lime tree in front of the window.
The lame lone dog wandering outside the summer house.
How much you had studied the silence by the side of the dead
    firemen,
their helmets fallen on the yellow grass! You had kept
the garden's rubber hose clean of any spots. The blind man
struck the pebbles with his rod, then the water. He understood,
    turned back. Then
you offered to direct him to the sidewalk opposite. But he
refused, quietly. He smiled at you, took off his hat
and gave you three playing cards he had hidden there.
But you knew nothing. You were a surgeon.

Kálamos, 10/22/72

ΜΙΑ ΠΟΡΤΑ

Δίπλα στὸ δρόμο ἡ θεόρατη τριγωνικὴ καγκελόπορτα,
ὁλότελα μόνη, δίχως κῆπο ἢ σπίτι. Πίσω της
τὸ πιὸ μεγάλο σύννεφο, γαλάζιο, μὲ τὸ μαῦρο τόξο
στ' ἀριστερὸ πλευρό του. Ὥστε, λοιπόν,—εἶπε ὁ γέρος—
δὲν εἶναι δίχως νόημα τὸ ποὺ δὲν ἔχεις τίποτα.

Κάλαμος, 22.Χ.72

A DOOR

Alongside the street an enormous triangular iron gate
utterly alone, without a garden or a house. Behind it,
the biggest of clouds, blue, with a black arch
on its left side. Well then — said the old man —
it's not meaningless to know *where* it is you have nothing.

Kálamos, 10/22/72

Ο ΑΛΛΟΣ

Εἴχαμε μιὰ κιθάρα, ἕνα μαχαίρι, τρεῖς παράταιρες καρέκλες.
Πάνω σὲ μιὰ ἐφημερίδα καθαρίζαμε βραστὲς πατάτες.
Ἡ γυναίκα μ᾽ ἕνα χερὶ κατέβαινε τὴ σκάλα. Ἀπὸ πάνω
χτυποῦσε ὁ κουτσὸς τὰ δεκανίκια του. Ὁ ἄλλος, μονάχος,
καθόταν στὴ γωνιά, παράμερα. Δὲν ἔτρωγε. Κοιτοῦσε τὰ νύχια του.
Ζητοῦσε νὰ πετύχει μιὰ μεγέθυνση, μιὰ θετικὴ παραμόρφωση,
μιὰ παρομοίωση ἔστω, νὰ ξεκόψει ἀπ᾽ τὰ λόγια μας, νὰ εἰσδύσει
μὲς στὸ ρυθμὸ ἢ στὴν ἐπιφάνεια τοῦ ρυθμοῦ, κυματίζοντας
σὰν τὸ κομμένο καὶ στυμμένο λεμόνι πάνω στὸ ποτάμι
μαζὶ μὲ τὸ μισὸ φεγγάρι, πλάϊ στὸ ξύλινο ὁμοίωμα τοῦ πνιγμένου,
ἐνῶ στὶς ὄχθες οἱ ἄνθρωποι χειρονομοῦσαν, φώναζαν, τρέχαν—
αὐτοὶ ποὺ βάζαν μεγαλύτερα χρέη νὰ ξοφλήσουν μικρότερα χρέη
καὶ ξόδευαν κι αὐτὰ κ᾽ ἐκεῖνα δίχως νὰ ξοφλήσουνε κανένα.

Ἀθήνα, 23.X.72

THE OTHER MAN

We had a guitar, a knife, three unmatched chairs,
and were peeling boiled potatoes on a newspaper.
The woman with a candle was descending the stairs. From above
the lame man was striking the floor with his crutches. The other
    man, alone,
sat in a corner apart. He wasn't eating. He was looking at his nails,
trying to achieve an enlargement, a positive disfigurement,
a resemblance at least, to break away from our words, to penetrate
into rhythm or into the surface of rhythm, undulating
like the cut and squeezed lemon floating on the river
together with the half moon, beside the wooden likeness of the
    drowned man,
while on the riverbanks men were gesticulating, shouting, running —
men who were amassing great debts to pay off smaller debts
and spending both these and those without paying off any.

Athens, 10/23/72

ΕΠΙΣΤΡΩΜΑΤΑ

Αὐτὰ τὰ σκοτεινὰ ἀντικείμενα, πιὸ μέσα εἶναι γαλάζια, καὶ πιὸ
μέσα τίποτα.
Ὡς ἐκεῖ, βέβαια, δὲν μπορεῖς νὰ φτάσεις—ἤ, μᾶλλον, δὲ θέλεις·
ἀφήνεις τὰ μεγάφωνα στὴ μεγαλύτερη ἔντασή τους,—δὲν ἀκοῦς
    διόλου·
μόνο κοιτάζεις στὴ μικρὴν ὀθόνη κεῖνο τὸ μεγάλο χέρι, ρωμαλέο,
δασύτριχο, μ' ἄψογα νύχια, νὰ κρεμάει στὸ πρατήριο τῆς βενζίνας
τὸ καμπύλο, μετάλλινο ἐπιστόμιο τοῦ σωλήνα. Στὸν καρπό του
ἔχει μιὰ πέτσινη φαρδειὰ μαύρη ταινία μὲ τρεῖς κρίκους
    νικελένιους.

Ἀθήνα, 22.X.72

LAYERS

These dark objects are blue within, and still further in are nothing.
As far as that, of course, you cannot reach — or rather, you don't
    want to;
you turn up the loudspeakers to their highest pitch — you can't
    hear a thing,
but only stare at that large hand on the television screen, sturdy,
thick-haired, with faultless fingernails, that on the gas station's
    pump was hanging
the rubber hose's curved metallic spigot. On its wrist
is a broad black leather belt with three links made of nickel.

                        Athens, 10/22/72

ΑΥΤΟΣ

Αὐτός, αὐτός,—τὸ ποδήλατο, τὸ μαχαίρι, τὸ ψάρι.
Ἄσ᾽ τον νὰ φύγει. Τὸ κίτρινο τρέμει στὴν κουρτίνα.
Ἀπ᾽ τὸ πρωΐ περπατοῦσε ξυπόλυτος στὸ προαύλιο
πάνω στὶς παγωμένες πλάκες·—ἥσυχος εἶταν·
ἔκανε πὼς κοιτάει ἀλλοῦ, κατὰ τοὺς λόφους. Αὐτὸς
μὲ τοὺς κρυμμένους ἀριθμοὺς τῶν πράξεών μας. Νά τος
αὐτός, παιδί μου. Πάψε πιά. Λάθος ἔκανα. Αὐτός,
αὐτὸς τὸ ψάρι, τὸ μαχαίρι, τὸ κίτρινο. Πῆρα τὸ ποδήλατο
μ᾽ ἕνα ψωμὶ καὶ δυὸ φτερά. Μὴν πεῖς ποῦ πῆγα.
Στὴ φλούδα τῆς μουριᾶς ἔχω χαράξει τὸ σημάδι.

Ἀθήνα, 23.X.72

116

HE

He, he — the bicycle, the knife, the fish.
Let him leave. The yellow in the curtains trembles.
Since morning he's been walking barefoot on the frozen tiles
of the front yard — he was calm,
pretending to be looking elsewhere, toward the hills. He
with the hidden numbers of our deeds. There,
that's him, my child. Stop now. I've made a mistake. He,
he, the fish, the knife, the yellow. I took the bicycle,
with a loaf of bread and two wings. Don't tell them where I've gone.
On the bark of the mulberry tree I've carved the sign.

Athens, 10/23/72

117

ΚΟΙΝΑ ΘΑΥΜΑΤΑ

Βγάλαν τὰ μανουάλια στὸ ὕπαιθρο, κάτω ἀπ' τὰ δέντρα.
Σφουγγάρισαν τὴν ἐκκλησία. Ἀπ' τὴ μεγάλη πόρτα
χυνόταν ἔξω ἡ σκοτεινὴ ὑγρασία στὰ σκαλοπάτια
καὶ στὶς ἄσπρες ἡλιόλουστες πλάκες. Ὁ καντηλανάφτης
κλώτσησε τὸ σκυλὶ ποὺ κουτσαίνοντας εἶχε σιμώσει
νὰ πιεῖ νερὸ ἀπ' τὸν κάδο. Τότε, ἀπ' τὴν ὡραία πύλη,
βγῆκε ὁ ἀρχάγγελος μὲ τὶς μεγάλες, κόκκινες φτεροῦγες,
ἔσκυψε στὸ σκυλί, καὶ τοῦδωσε νὰ πιεῖ ἀπ' τὶς φοῦχτες του.
Ἔτσι περπάτησαν τὴν ἄλλη μέρα οἱ πέντε παραλυτικοί.

Ἀθήνα, 23.Χ.72

COMMON MIRACLES

They took out the candelabra into the open air under the trees
and scrubbed the church. From the large door
a dark humidity spread out over the steps
and over the white sunwashed tiles. The beadle
kicked a limping dog that had drawn near
to drink water from the bucket. Then, from the beautiful altar door,
the Archangel with his large red wings came out,
stooped to the dog, and gave it to drink out of his cupped hands.
And so the next day the five paralytics walked.

Athens, 10/23/72

119

Η ΠΑΡΑΦΩΝΗ ΣΥΓΧΟΡΔΙΑ

Ἔτσι, ξανά, ξανά, τὴ συγχορδία ἐτούτη, νὰ πυκνώσει ὁ χρόνος,
νὰ σταθεῖ τὸ σκοτάδι, νὰ μὴν ἁπλώσει. Τὸ φαλακρὸ κεφάλι
ποῦσπασε τὴν κατάφωτη βιτρίνα τοῦ χρυσοχοείου
νὰ μείνει ἐκεῖ, σφηνωμένο, μὲ τὸ ἀκάνθινο στεφάνι
ἀπὸ σπασμένα κρύσταλλα· καὶ στὸ φαρδύ, σκυμμένο αὐχένα
νὰ φαίνεται τὸ αἷμα ποὺ ἀνεβαίνει, στριμώχνεται, σφύζει
περιχαράζοντας τὴν ἄσπρη οὐλὴ ἀπ' τὴν ἀρχαία λαβωματιά.

'Αθήνα, 24.Χ.72

THE DISSONANT CHORD

Thus, again and again, this chord, that time may thicken,
that darkness may stop, that it may not spread. Let the bald head
that broke the lit window of the jewelry shop
remain there, wedged, with its thorny crown
of shattered crystals; and on its broad, bent nape
let the blood be seen as it mounts, swells, throbs
and traces out the white scar of the ancient wound.

Athens, 10/24/72

ΠΟΛΛΑΠΛΑΣΙΑΣΜΟΣ ΤΟΥ ΑΓΝΩΣΤΟΥ

Μίλησα—λέει—στὸν τοῖχο, μίλησα στὰ δοκάρια. Φώναξα «ναί»,
ν᾽ ἀκούσουν, νὰ τὸ ξαναποῦν, νὰ τ᾽ ἀκούσω. Ἄχ, μαῦρα κουπιά μου
ἀπ᾽ τὰ μεγάλα μαῦρα δέντρα μου. Ἀκούω τὰ βράδια
τ᾽ ἄγριο χλιμίντρισμα τοῦ ἀλόγου ἀπ᾽ τὸν ἀντίκρυ κινηματογράφο·
γλυστροῦν στ᾽ ἄσπρο πανὶ τὰ ὑποβρύχια ἐλάφια. Τὴ νύχτα,—
τί μεθυσμένη νύχτα,—τὸ χνῶτο της ἀφήνει στὶς κουρτίνες
μαβιὲς καὶ κόκκινες κηλίδες. Ὁ θάνατος—εἶπε—
εἶναι κρυμμένος στὶς ἀρβύλες τῶν στρατιωτῶν. Ἕνας,
δεύτερος, τρίτος, δέκατος, ἔβδομος, κ᾽ ἐγώ·—πόσες καὶ πόσες
διαδοχικὲς ἀποστασίες. Δὲ γνωρίζω κανέναν. Φύγαν
ἀφήνοντάς μου στὸ μαρμάρινο τραπέζι τὶς ταυτότητές τους
νὰ ψάχνω, νὰ μὴ βρίσκω τί εἶταν, τί εἶμαι, τί εἶναι,—
καὶ τοῦτες οἱ φωτογραφίες κάθε μέρα πιὸ μόνες, πιὸ ξένες,
πλάϊ στ᾽ ἀνοιχτὸ ψαλίδι, στὴν πυξίδα, στὴ σιωπή, στὸ στυλό μου.

Ἀθήνα, 24.X.72

AUGMENTATION OF THE UNKNOWN

I spoke — he said — to the wall, I spoke to the rafters, I shouted
    "Yes,"
so they could hear it, so they could repeat it, so I could hear it.
    Ah, my black oars
from my large black trees. At night I hear
the horse's wild whinnying from the movie house opposite;
the submarine deer glide on the white screen. The breath
of a night — what a drunken night — leaves on the curtains
blue and red stains. Death — he said —
is hidden in the soldier's boots. One,
a second, third, tenth, eleventh, and I — how many
successive apostates. I don't know anyone. They went away,
leaving me their identity cards on the marble table
to search and not to find what they were, what I am —
and these photographs more alone day by day, more alien,
beside the open scissors, the compass, the silence, my pen.

Athens, 10/24/72

ΑΝΩΝΥΜΟΣ ΔΡΟΜΟΣ

Βγαίνουν δυὸ - δυό, ἕνας - ἕνας ἀπ' τὴν πόρτα οἱ μεθυσμένοι·
σκοντάφτουν στοὺς σπάγγους τῆς νύχτας. Λίγο πιὸ κάτω
εἶναι τὸ καφενεῖο τῶν σιδηροδρομικῶν, ὁ φοῦρνος, τὸ κουρεῖο
μὲ τοὺς δυὸ ταριχευμένους πελαργοὺς πάνω στὸ ράφι. Ἡ γυναίκα
κοντοστάθηκε λίγο στὸ δρόμο. Κοίταξε τὴ βιτρίνα
τοῦ φωταγωγημένου κλειστοῦ ἰχθυοπωλείου. Στὰ φαρδιὰ πανέρια
σαλεύανε τὰ πεθαμένα ψάρια (ἄλλα σταχτιά, ἄλλα κόκκινα)
καθὼς ἀνάμεσά τους ἔλιωναν τὰ κομμάτια τοῦ πάγου. Ἡ γυναίκα
ἔβγαλε τότε τὸν μικρὸ καθρέφτη καὶ κοιτάχτηκε—
τὄνα της μάτι εἶταν σταχτί, τ' ἄλλο κόκκινο. Χαχογέλασε
ἕτοιμη πιὰ ν' ἀποκριθεῖ· ὅμως κανεὶς δὲν εἶταν νὰ ρωτήσει.

Ἀθήνα, 24.Χ.72

124

ANONYMOUS STREET

The drunks came out the door one by one and two by two,
stumbling over the strings of night. A little farther down
lay the railroad workers' coffee house, the bakery, the barber shop
with its two stuffed storks on a shelf. The woman
paused a while in the street. She looked at the illuminated
shop window of the closed fish store. In wide baskets
the dead fish stirred (some red, some the color of ash)
as the crushed ice between them melted. Then the woman
took out her small mirror and looked at herself —
one of her eyes was red, the other the color of ash. She smiled,
ready to answer at last, but there was no one there to ask.

                                        Athens, 10/24/72

ΑΝΑΝΕΩΜΕΝΗ ΑΘΩΟΤΗΤΑ

Τὸ πρωΐ, κατὰ τὶς 10, 6γαίνουν οἱ καχεκτικὲς γυναῖκες
ἀπ᾽ τὴ μικρὴ κουζίνα τους ἀμίλητες· πηγαίνουν στὸ φοῦρνο
τὸ ταψὶ τὶς πατάτες. Δὲν ξαναγυρίζουν. Οἱ ἄλλες γυναῖκες,
τὴν ἴδια ὥρα περίπου, 6γαίνουν ἀπ᾽ τὸ φοῦρνο, κρατώντας
ἕνα ζεστὸ ψωμὶ στὴ μασκάλη τους. Βιάζονται. Ἀνηφορίζουν
ὣς στὸ σταθμὸ τοῦ τραίνου. Δὲ φαίνονται πιά. Ἴσως περάσαν
τὴν ὑπόγεια διάβασῃ μὲ τοὺς τυφλοὺς ζητιάνους. Ἴσως σταθῆκαν
χαζεύοντας τὰ ἐξώφυλλα τῶν περιοδικῶν στὸ περίπτερο
μ᾽ ἐκεῖνες τὶς ξένες γυμνές. Τὸ πιθανότερο, ὅμως
εἶναι νὰ τράβηξαν ἴσα στὸν οὐρανὸ πρὶν κρυώσει τὸ ψωμί τους.
   Τώρα
τὰ τρία πλανόδια σκυλιὰ θεονήστικα, σκυφτά, ἀδυνατισμένα
κλαῖνε μπροστὰ στὴ μάντρα μὲ τὰ σπασμένα γυαλικά. Κ᾽ ἐγὼ
δὲν ξέρω τίποτα πιά, τόσο ποὺ ὅπου κι ἂν κοιτάξω ἕνα γύρω,
τὴ σκάλα, τὸ φανάρι, τὸ καρφὶ τοῦ τοίχου, ἀνακαλύπτω ἕνα θαῦμα.

Ἀθήνα, 25.Χ.72

RENEWED INNOCENCE

In the morning about ten the sickly women come out
of the small kitchen silently, each taking to the baker's oven
a tray filled with potatoes. They do not return. Other women,
about the same time, come out of the baker's shop, each holding
a warm loaf of bread under her armpit. They're in a hurry. They
    walk uphill
as far as the railroad station. They can no longer be seen. Perhaps
they went through the underpass with the blind beggars. Perhaps
    they paused
to loiter by the newsstand before the magazine covers
with foreign, naked women. It's most likely, however,
they made straight for the sky before their bread got cold. Now
the three vagabond dogs, starved, stooped, and spindly,
weep before the wall with its broken glass. And I
no longer know a thing, so much so that wherever I look about me,
at the stairs, the lantern, the nail on the wall, I detect a miracle.

Athens, 10/25/72

ΣΑΝ ΠΡΟΣΕΥΧΗ

Ἄφησέ τους ἀκόμη μιὰ μέρα μὲ τὶς μικρές τους λέξεις,
μὲ τοὺς μικροὺς περιπατητικοὺς θανάτους, Νοέμβρης μῆνας,
κάτω ἀπ' τὰ λίγα, ὁλόχρυσα δέντρα. Τὸ παλιὸ καράβι
ἀράζει πίσω ἀπ' τὰ βράχια, στὸν ἀπόκρυφο ὅρμο·
βγάζουνε τοὺς ἀμίλητους ἀρρώστους σκυθρωποὶ χωροφυλάκοι
γιὰ νὰ τοὺς κλείσουν στὸ λεπροκομεῖο. Θέ μου. Τί μόνοι,
τί ξένοι ὁ ἕνας στὸν ἄλλον,—τόσο ὅμοιοι, νὰ πιαστοῦν ἀπ' τοὺς
    ὤμους
καὶ νὰ χορέψουν κεῖνο τὸ ἀργοπάτητο ξεχασμένο τραγούδι:
μαῦρα μου κυπαρίσσια, μαῦρα σύννεφα, μαῦρο ψωμί μου κι ἁλάτι.

'Αθήνα, 25.Χ.72

128

LIKE A PRAYER

Permit them one more day with their small words,
their small peripatetic deaths, in the month of November
under the few gold-glimmering trees. The old ship
moors behind the rocks in the secret bay,
discharging its silent sick, its somber gendarmes,
to be locked up in the leper house. Dear God, how alone they are,
what strangers to one another — so alike, grasping one another by
    the shoulders
and dancing to that sluggish and forgotten song:
my black cypress tree, black clouds, my black bread and salt.

Athens, 10/25/72

ΑΠΟΧΡΩΣΕΙΣ ΕΝΟΣ ΣΥΝΝΕΦΟΥ

Μόνος κ' ἐκεῖνο τὸ ἀπόγευμα. ῏Ω κόκκινο σύννεφο,—εἶπε—
ἐσὺ ποὺ μοὖβαψες κόκκινα τὰ χέρια, δὲν ἔμαθα ποιὸς φταίει,
ἴσως κανείς, ἴσως μονάχα ἐγώ. ᾽Εγὼ εἴμουν ποὺ εἶδα
νὰ χάνεται στὴ σκόνη τοῦ δρόμου τὸ μικρὸ παιδὶ τοῦ μουγγοῦ,
μουγγὸ κι αὐτὸ—αὐτὸ ποὺ πουλοῦσε χάρτινες σημαιοῦλες
τῶν ποδοσφαιρικῶν ἀγώνων, ὑψώνοντας τὄνα δάχτυλό του
νὰ δείχνει τὴν τιμὴ τῆς μιᾶς δραχμῆς, κ' ἴσως νὰ δείχνει
κάτι πολὺ ψηλότερα ποὺ δὲν μποροῦσα νὰ δῶ. Τότε πλησιάσαν
οἱ δυὸ μοτοσυκλέτες, τὸν βάλαν στὴ μέση, τοῦ δέσαν τὰ χέρια,
τοῦ πέταξαν τὶς σημαιοῦλες, τὶς σκόρπισε ὁ ἀέρας, πρόφτασα
καὶ πῆρα μιὰ χωρὶς νὰ τὴν πληρώσω. Τότε κατάλαβα
τὴν τιμὴ πούδειχνε μὲ τὸ ὑψωμένο δάχτυλό του. ῏Ω σύννεφο,
κόκκινο σύννεφο ποὺ μοὖβαψες κόκκινα τὰ χέρια, ἐσὺ
ποὺ γύρισες πρὸς τὸ μενεξελὶ μὲ δυὸ χρυσὲς φτεροῦγες.

᾽Αθήνα, 25.Χ.72

130

HUES OF A CLOUD

Alone that afternoon also. O red cloud — he said —
you who have dyed my hands red, I've not learned who's to
    blame;
perhaps no one, perhaps only I. It was I who saw
the mute's small boy vanishing in the dust of the street,
himself a mute — the one who used to sell small paper flags
of each soccer team, raising one finger
to point out the price of one drachma, and perhaps pointing out
something much higher which I could not see. Then two on
    motorcycles
approached him, placed him in the middle, tied his hands together,
threw away his little flags, which the air scattered till I grabbed one
without paying for it. It was then I understood
the price he was pointing out with his raised finger. O cloud,
red cloud who have dyed my hand red, you
who have turned toward violet with two golden wings.

                                        Athens, 10/25/72

131

ΔΙΑΚΟΠΗ ΗΛΕΚΤΡΙΚΟΥ ΡΕΥΜΑΤΟΣ

Ἐκεῖνο τὸ ἀπειλητικὸ σκοτεινὸ βράδι πετρωμένο μπροστὰ στὶς τζα-
μόπορτες.
Σβησμένη ἡ γέφυρα. Τὸ ζαχαροπλαστεῖο, τὸ τσιμεντάδικο, ἡ πόλη.
Ποῦ νἆναι
τὰ σπαρματσέτα ἀπ᾽ τὶς ἀρρώστιες τῶν παιδιῶν; Ποῦ ᾽ναι τὰ σπίρτα;
Ποῦ ᾽ναι τὰ χέρια ποὺ μποροῦσαν νὰ ψάχνουν; Μὴ σέρνεις λοιπὸν τὴν
καρέκλα.
Μὴν πᾶς πρὸς τὰ κεῖ,—τὸ σκοτεινότερο σημεῖο εἶναι ἡ σκάλα. Ἀπ᾽
ἔξω
ἕνα τεράστιο μαῦρο - μαῦρο πιάνο μὲ σωπασμένη μουσική, πατώντας
μὲ τὰ τρία του πόδια τὶς ἀντίστοιχες γωνιὲς τῆς πολιτείας·
ἡ τέταρτη γωνιὰ ἀκατοίκητη·—μὲς ἀπ᾽ αὐτὴ ἀκριβῶς ἀκούγεται
τὸ ἀμεταποίητο κενὸ μαζὶ μὲ τὸν ἀμεταποίητο φόβο, μήπως δὲν εἶναι
πραγματικὰ κενό· μήπως ἐκεῖ μένει κρυμμένη, παρακολουθώντας
μας,
ἡ δεύτερη γυναίκα μὲ τὰ κίτρινα γάντια, ὅπως ἡ πρώτη μὲ τὰ μαῦρα.

Ἀθήνα, 26.Χ.72

THE ELECTRIC CURRENT CUT OFF

That threatening dark evening petrified before the glass doors.
The bridge, the candy shop, the cement factory, the city, all oblit-
    erated. Where are
the candles from the children's illnesses? Where are the matches?
Where are the hands capable of searching? Well then, don't drag
    the chair.
Don't go in that direction — the darkest spot is the stair. Outside
there's an enormous jet-black piano with silenced music, stepping
with its three legs on the corresponding corners of the city;
the fourth corner is uninhabited — it's precisely out of this
that the unalterable void is heard together with the unalterable
    fear. Perhaps
it's not truly a void — perhaps within it lies hidden, watching us,
the second woman with the yellow gloves, like the first woman
    with the black.

                                        Athens, 10/26/72

ΤΕΤΑΡΤΟ ΝΥΧΤΕΡΙΝΟ

Ἡ νύχτα—μᾶς ἔλεγε—εἶναι ἄρρωστη, (σὰ νἄταν στ' ἀλήθεια
ἕνα μικρὸ κορίτσι ἢ μιὰ γυναίκα), πολὺ ἄρρωστη—ἔλεγε·
οὔτε κ' ἡ πιὸ λυπημένη μητέρα δὲν μπορεῖ νὰ τῆς ἀγγίξει
τὸ χέρι ἢ τὰ μαλλιά. Οἱ δρομεῖς ἐπιστρέφουν. Στὶς βιτρίνες
τῶν συνοικιακῶν φωτογραφείων, κάτω ἀπ' τὰ ὠχρὰ λαμπιόνια,
χαμογελοῦν οἱ νεόνυμφες μὲ πολύπτυχα πέπλα, νοικιασμένα
ἀπ' τὴν ἱματιοθήκη τοῦ κλειστοῦ θεάτρου, ἀπὸ κεῖ ποὺ νοικιάζουν
κάθε ἀποκριὰ κορδέλες, ντέφια, νυχτικιὲς δαντελένιες
γιὰ τ' ἄλογα τὰ χαρτονένια, τὶς μικρὲς μαϊμοῦδες, τὶς ἀρκοῦδες
κ' ἕνα φαρδὺ χασεδένιο κοστούμι μὲ μαῦρα σειρήτια γιὰ μένα.

Ἀθήνα, 26.Χ.72

FOURTH NOCTURNE

The night — he would say — is sick (as though it were in truth
a small girl or a woman), very sick — he would say;
not even the saddest mother is able to touch
her hand or her hair. The runners return. In the windows
of every neighborhood photography shop, under the pale streetlamps,
smile newly-wed brides with their pleated veils, rented
from the wardrobe of the closed theater from which, during every
    carnival season,
ribbons are rented, tambourines, lace nightgowns
for paper horses, small monkeys, bears,
and a wide calico costume with black bands just for me.

Athens, 10/26/72

ΜΟΝΑΧΙΚΗ ΟΜΙΛΙΑ

Πιὸ φόβος εἶναι ὁ ὕπνος, σκοντάφτοντας στὸ ἀνασκαμμένο χῶμα
σὲ διάλειμμα πολέμου. Ἐδῶ ν' ἀργοπορήσεις, πλάϊ στὸ φανοστάτη,
ἔξω ἀπ' τ' ἀνθοπωλεῖο, ξενοίκιαστο μῆνες καὶ μῆνες τώρα. Ἐδῶ
οἱ ἄλλοι δὲ βλέπουν. Κάνε πὼς ψάχνεις τὴ χαμένη δεκάρα
ἢ τὸ κλειδὶ τῆς βαλίτσας σου. Στὸ γωνιακὸ φωτισμένο καφενεῖο
φαίνεται πίσω ἀπ' τὰ τζάμια ὁ ποδοσφαιριστὴς τῆς γειτονιᾶς τριγυ-
ρισμένος
ἀπ' τοὺς μικροὺς θαυμαστές του. Στ' ἄλλο τραπέζι τρεῖς ἄντρες μὲ
ψαλίδια
κόβουν σὲ κύκλους κίτρινα χαρτόνια. Τὸ γκαρσόνι, ὀρθὸ στὸ
μεσότοιχο,
μοιάζει ὀργισμένο. Ἡ γυναίκα κοιμᾶται στὸ ταμεῖο. Τὴν ἴδια νύχτα
εἶταν πού, λίγο πάρα κάτω, στὴ μικρὴ πλατεία, μιὰ παρέα μεθυσμένοι
πάσκιζαν νὰ περάσουνε στὰ πόδια τοῦ πεσμένου ἀγάλματος
δυὸ λασπωμένες γαλότσες·—τ' ἄγαλμα ἐκεῖνο ποὺ παράσταινε ἐσένα.

'Αθήνα, 26.Χ.72

136

SOLITARY DISCOURSE

More fearful is sleep, stumbling over the excavated earth
in an interval of war. Walk slowly here, beside the lamppost
outside the flower shop unrented now month after month. Here.
The others don't see. Pretend you're searching for a lost dime
or the key to your suitcase. In the lit corner coffee house
the neighborhood's soccer player can be seen surrounded
by his small admirers. At the other table three men with scissors
are cutting yellow cardboard into circles. The waiter, standing
    upright by the partition,
seems to be in a rage. The woman at the cashier's desk is sleep-
    ing. It was
on that same night, a little further down in the small town square,
    that a party of drunks
tried to shoe the feet of the fallen statue there
with two muddy galoshes — of that statue there portraying you!

Athens, 10/26/72

137

ΑΠΟΣΙΩΠΗΣΕΙΣ

Μέσα στοὺς σκοτεινοὺς θαλάμους τῶν φωτογραφείων
τ' ἀρνητικὰ τῆς νύχτας καὶ ἡ ἄγρια μαύρη γυναίκα
κατάλευκη σὰν ἄγαλμα σὲ κατάλευκο βάθος, ἐνῶ
οἱ φωτογραφικὲς μηχανὲς τῶν δημοσιογράφων
μένουν παρατημένες στὰ τραπέζια, στὶς καρέκλες,
καὶ μία, ἡ πιὸ μεγάλη, κάτω ἀπ' τὸ κρεββάτι
ὅπου, γυμνός, εἶναι κρυμμένος ὁ ἀγγελιοφόρος.

Ἀθήνα, 26.Χ.72

RETICENCE

In the photographer's dark rooms are
the negatives of night and a wild black woman
as pure white as a statue against a pure white background, while
the photographic machines of the reporters
lie abandoned on the tables, on the chairs,
and one of them, the largest of all, is under the bed
where, stark naked, the messenger lies hidden.

Athens, 10/26/72

ΣΙΩΠΗΛΟ ΕΓΚΩΜΙΟ

(στὰ 75χρονα τοῦ ΑΡΑΓΚΟΝ)

Αὐτὸς μὲ μιὰ κόμη ἀπὸ ἄσπρη φωτιά, μὲ τὴν ἀκραία κομψότητα
    τοῦ ἀρνούμενου,
μὲ τὶς πολύτιμες ἀντανακλάσεις φωταγωγημένων ἀεροδρομίων
σὲ κάθε νύχι τοῦ χεριοῦ του—Ποῦ πᾶς ἔτσι μόνος—εἶπε ὁ ἄλλος—
σὲ τούτη τὴν ἀτέλειωτη ὄχθη, κάτω ἀπ᾽ τοὺς σταυροὺς ξεγυμνωμένων
    δέντρων,
πλάϊ στὸ μαῦρο ποτάμι, προσεχτικός, ἀπρόσεχτος, ταΐζοντας μὲ
    μεγάλα διαμάντια
βιαστικά, ἀνυποψίαστα ψάρια;—ἐσὺ ποὺ ἔσμιξες ὅλα τ᾽ ἀντίθετα στὸν
    ἔναν ρυθμό. Ποῦ πᾶς, λοιπόν,
ἔτσι μονάχος, παρασημοφορημένος, μὲς στὴ θλίψη μακρινῶν
    ἐπευφημιῶν; Τὸ ξέρω
μέσα στὴν τσέπη τοῦ κ α ι ν ο ύ ρ γ ι ο υ βελουδένιου σακκακιοῦ σου
    (γι᾽ αὐτὸ πιὸ λ υ π η μ έ ν ο υ)
κρατᾶς κρυμμένο ὄχι τὸ μέτρο τοῦ ἀρχαίου Ξυλουργοῦ, ἀλλὰ τὸ ἔνα
ἀτσάλινο πτυσσόμενο φτερό σου. Τὸ δεύτερο δὲν κρύβεται· αὐτὸ
σοῦ σκιάζει τὰ δυὸ τρίτα τοῦ προσώπου σου καὶ τὸ μαβὶ πουκάμισό
    σου
κάτω ἀπ᾽ τοὺς προβολεῖς τῆς ἀγέρωχης νύχτας. Ἀπ᾽ τὸν ἴσκιο
αὐτοῦ ἀκριβῶς τοῦ φτεροῦ σ᾽ ἀναγνωρίζουν τ᾽ ἀγάλματα, οἱ ποιητές,
    οἱ φοιτητές, ἡ ἐπανάσταση κ᾽ ἐγώ. Ὅμως ἐγὼ
καλύτερα ἀπ᾽ ὅλους σὲ γνωρίζω, ἀπ᾽ τὸ πρῶτο πτυσσόμενο, τὸ
    κρυμμένο φτερό.

Ἀθήνα, 27.X.72

140

SILENT PRAISE

On Aragon's 75th Year

He with hair of white fire, with the extreme elegance of one
    who denies,
with the precious reflections of illuminated airports
on each of his fingernails. Where are you going alone like this —
    said the other —
on this endless riverbank under the crosses of trees stripped bare,
next to the black river, carefully, carelessly, feeding large diamonds
to hurried and unsuspecting fish — you who merged all opposites
    into one rhythm? Where are you going, then,
alone like this, invested with many honors, in the sorrow of dis-
    tant acclamation? I know
that in the pocket of your *new* velvet coat (and for this reason
    much *sadder*)
you keep hidden, not the measuring tape of the ancient Carpenter,
    but your one
enfolded steel wing. The second one cannot be hidden, for it
shades two-thirds of your face and your dark blue shirt
under the floodlights of arrogant night. It's by the shadow
of precisely this wing that you can be recognized by statues,
    poets, students, the revolution and me. But I,
better than anyone else, know you by the first, folded, hidden
    wing.

Athens, 10/27/72

141

ΔΙΚΑΙΟΣΥΝΗ

Τὸ παρθεναγωγεῖο, τὸ τραῖνο, τὸ ἰχθυοτροφεῖο, τὸ νεκροταφεῖο,—
ἄνεργοι ἠθοποιοὶ γυρνοῦν στὰ καφενεῖα, βαμμένοι, μὲ περοῦκες
μεγάλων ρόλων ποὺ δὲν ἔπαιξαν. Στὸ μάρμαρο τοῦ τραπεζιοῦ μένουν
φλούδια ἀπὸ πασατέμπους καὶ κύκλοι ἁλατιοῦ ἀπ' τὰ ποτήρια. Ὁ
 πιανίστας
ὅταν σβήνουν τὰ φῶτα ἐπιστρέφει ξυπόλυτος στὴν αἴθουσα τῶν
 ἐπισήμων·
κοιμᾶται μὲς στὸ πιάνο, σηκώνεται τὸ χάραμα. Φεύγει κάτω ἀπ'
 τὰ δέντρα
τυλιγμένος ὁλόκληρος σὲ ἄγραφες μουσικὲς σελίδες. Τότε εἴταν ποὺ ὁ
 Παῦλος:
τὸ κρυφὸ «θέλω»—εἶχε πεῖ—εἶναι «μπορῶ». Θυμηθεῖτε κεῖνες τὶς
 νύχτες
ποὺ οἱ σφαῖρες σφύριζαν δίπλα στ' αὐτιά μας, πέφταν στὸν καθρέφτη
κι ὁ καθρέφτης δὲν ἔσπαζε· γέμιζε τρύπες. Μὲς ἀπ' αὐτὲς τὶς τρύπες
ὅγάζαν τὰ χέρια τους οἱ σκοτωμένοι καὶ μᾶς παῖρναν τὸ ψωμὶ ἀπ' τὸ
 στόμα
γιατὶ κι αὐτοὶ πεινοῦν κι ἄλλο δὲν ἔχουν ἀπ' τὰ ἄσπρα τους δόντια.

'Αθήνα, 27.Χ.72

JUSTICE

The girl's school, the train, the fishery, the cemetery —
unemployed actors loiter in the coffee houses, all made up, wear-
    ing the wigs
of great roles they have never played. On the marble tabletop lie
the husks of roasted pumpkin seeds and salt rings left by glasses.
    When the lights
are switched off, the pianist returns barefooted to the hall of the
    officials,
sleeps in the piano, gets up at daybreak, and slips away under the
    trees,
wrapped completely in unscored music sheets. And then Paul spoke:
The secret of "I want" — he said — is "I can." Recall those nights
when the bullets whistled close to our ears; they'd fall on the mirror,
and the mirror would not shatter, but fill with holes. Out of these
    holes
the slain thrust out their hands and snatched away the bread out
    of our mouths,
because they too were hungry and had nothing more than their
    white teeth.

Athens, 10/27/72

143

Η ΙΔΙΑ ΚΡΑΥΓΗ

Θὰ φωνάξω—λέει—ἀκόμη μιὰ φορά· θὰ τοὺς φωνάξω «σιωπή»·
θὰ βγάλω ἀπ' τὴν κορνίζα τὴ φωτογραφία τοῦ πιὸ παλιοῦ προγόνου·
θὰ μπῶ μὲς στὴν κορνίζα ἐγὼ μὲ τὸ τσιγάρο μου. Στὴ
    ράχη μου θᾶχω
τὸ ἴδιο σκεβρωμένο, μουχλιασμένο χαρτόνι, καρφωμένο
μὲ τὰ μικρὰ σκουριασμένα καρφιά. Ἐκεῖ, ξεχασμένος,
μὲ συντροφιὰ τὶς ἀράχνες καὶ τὶς λίγες κούφιες μύγες,
μπροστὰ στοὺς δώδεκα κωφάλαλους ποὺ μὲ κοιτοῦν στὰ μάτια
νὰ τοὺς φωνάξω πάλι «σιωπή», παρ' ὅτι ξέρω πώς, καὶ τώρα,
μὲς στὰ χειροκροτήματά τους, ἡ φωνή μου δὲ θ' ἀκουστεῖ.

                                        Ἀθήνα, 27.Χ.72

THE SAME SHOUT

I will shout — he said — one more time; I will shout to them, "Be
    quiet!"
I will take the photograph of the oldest ancestor out of its frame
and enter into the frame myself with my cigarette. On my back I
    shall carry
the same warped, mouldy cardboard, studded
with small rusty nails. There, forgotten,
with spiders and a few hollow flies for company,
in front of the twelve deaf-mutes who stare into my eyes,
I'll shout to them again, "Be quiet!", although I know that, even
    now,
amid their applause, my voice will not be heard.

Athens, 10/27/72

145

ΕΠΙΤΗΡΗΣΗ

Μὴ στρέφεις πίσω, μὴν κοιτάξεις μπροστά, μὴ μείνεις
ἀνάμεσα στὰ δύο, ἐκεῖ ἢ ἐδῶ. Μαῦροι λεκέδες στὶς λεωφόρους.
Τραγούδια καὶ σημαῖες στριμωγμένα στὰ τραῖνα. Μιὰ κουβέρτα
εἶχε πέσει στὶς ράγιες. Θὰ γυρίσουμε—εἶπαν. Δὲ γύρισαν. Τώρα
παπούτσια καὶ τσιγάρα κολλημένα στὴ λάσπη. Τίποτα,—λέει—
δὲν κερδίζεται τίποτα—μήτε μὲ τὸ αἷμα. Ἕνας ἄνθρωπος μόνος
κάθεται στὰ σκαλιὰ τῆς ἐκκλησίας, μισοκοιμᾶται· μὲς στὸ καπέλο
    του
ἔχει βάλει μιὰ πέτρα. Τί ξεχασμένα πράγματα, τί ἄσκοπα λόγια.
Ἕνας παλιὸς ἀργαλειὸς στὸν ἴσκιο τῆς μουριᾶς. Καὶ τὸ χρυσὸ πουλὶ
μὲ τὄνα πόδι καὶ τὶς δυὸ κεφαλὲς νὰ μᾶς κοιτάει ἕναν - ἕναν
ἀσάλευτο πάντα περιστρέφοντας μόνον τὴ γυάλινη ματιά του.

Κάλαμος, 28.X.72

SURVEILLANCE

Don't look back, don't look before you, don't remain
between the two, here or there. Black stains on the avenues.
Songs and flags crammed in the trains. A blanket
had fallen on the railroad track. We shall return — they said.
    They did not. Now
shoes and cigarettes stuck in the mud. Nothing — he says —
nothing is gained — not even with blood. One solitary man is
    sitting on the church stairs, half asleep; in his hat
he has placed a stone. What forgotten things, what aimless words.
An old loom in the shade of the mulberry tree. And the golden bird
with one foot and two heads looking at us one by one,
always motionless, turning round and round only its glassy eyes.

Kálamos, 10/27/72

Οἱ πυροβολισμοὶ εἶχαν σταματήσει πιά. Δὲν ἀκουγόταν τίποτα.
Τὰ παιδιὰ βγαῖναν ἀπ' τὸ ὑπόγειο, ἀργὰ τὸ ἀπόγευμα,
κοιτοῦσαν τὰ σπασμένα ποδήλατα. Σώπαιναν. Στὸ μπαλκόνι,
ἐκεῖ ποὺ κρέμονταν ὥς χτὲς ἀκόμα ἡ πιὸ μεγάλη σημαία,
μονάχα οἱ κουτσουλιὲς τῶν σπουργιτιῶν. Ἕνα θλιμμένο γερόντιο
πολὺ σκυφτό, στὸ ἀπέναντι παράθυρο, μὲ τὸ μεγάλο φακό του
παρατηροῦσε μιὰ κηλίδα στὸ σακκάκι του. Ὕστερα
βγάλανε βιαστικὰ τοὺς σκοτωμένους κ' ἔφυγαν τρέχοντας
σὰ νἄχαν κλέψει τὴν τεράστια μαύρη ἐξέδρα τοῦ δικαστηρίου.
Κάτω ἀπ' αὐτὴ τὴν ἐξέδρα εἶταν κρυμμένο τὸ παιδὶ μὲ τὰ πατίνια.

Κάλαμος, 28.Χ.72

32 YEARS

The firing had finally ceased. Nothing could be heard.
The children were coming out of the cellar, late in the afternoon,
looking at the broken bicycles. They fell silent. On the balcony
where even yesterday the largest flag was still hanging,
only sparrow droppings. A sad old man, hunched up,
with his large magnifying glass in the window opposite
was scrutinizing a large stain on his coat. Afterward,
they hurriedly took out the dead and left, running,
as if they had stolen the enormous black dais in the courtroom.
Under this dais the child with the roller skates had hidden.

Kálamos, 10/28/72

ΑΠΟΣΒΕΣΗ

Ἥσυχη θάλασσα πίσω ἀπ' τὰ τζάμια. Ἀναμενόμενο ποίημα.
Ἄσπρα, γυμνὰ κλωνάρια τῆς συκιᾶς μὲ μακριὰ νήματα
μιᾶς ξηλωμένης ναυτικῆς φανέλας. Πέρασαν δύο.
Ὁ ἕνας μ' ἐπίδεσμο στὸ μάτι. Ὁ ἄλλος διστάζοντας
μὲ τὸ φόβο τῆς ἐπανάληψης. Νὰ φύγει; Νὰ μείνει;
Μιὰ ξεχασμένη μυρωδιὰ μαζὶ μὲ κίτρινη σκόνη
βγαίνει ἀπ' τὴν πόρτα τοῦ πριονιστήριου. Κ' οἱ λέξεις—εἶπε—
οἱ ἐλάχιστες δικές μας, δίχως βάρος πιά, σὰν τὰ πούπουλα
μετὰ τὴν τουφεκιὰ τοῦ κυνηγοῦ νὰ πέφτουν στὸ βουβὸ ποτάμι.

Κάλαμος, 28.Χ.72

150

EXTINCTION

A tranquil sea behind the windowpanes. A poem expected.
White naked branches of the fig tree with long fibers
of an unraveled nautical sweater. Two passed by.
One with his eye bandaged. The other hesitating
with the fear of repetition. Should he leave? Should he remain?
A forgotten smell together with a yellow dust
drifts out the door of the sawmill. And the words — he said —
our slightest ones, without weight now, like down
falling on a mute river after a hunter's gunblast.

Kálamos, 10/28/72

ΔΡΑΠΕΤΕΥΣΗ

Βγαῖναν ἀπ᾽ τὸ λουτρώνα τοῦ ἀνθρακωρυχείου. Τὰ πόδια τους
λάμπαν.
Τὸ σκοτεινὸ φωτισμένο—πιὸ μυστικό· βρεγμένες πετσέτες
μὲ μαῦρες βοῦλλες στὰ πλακάκια τοῦ διαδρόμου. Δὲν ξέραν.
Τμηματικὲς παραστάσεις στοὺς καθρέφτες,—ἄλογα, δάση,
κ᾽ ἕνα κουτὶ σιδερένιο ἀφημένο στὸν ἴσκιο τοῦ βουνοῦ τὸ δείλι,
ἐγὼ μίλια πιὸ πέρα ἀπομακρύνονταν ἡ βάρκα μὲ τ᾽ ἄδεια καλάθια
σὲ μιὰ ἥσυχη, φλεγόμενη, ὁλοπόρφυρη θάλασσα μὲ κωπηλάτη
ἐκεῖνον τὸν ὡραῖον, ὁλόγυμνο δραπέτη τοῦ ψυχιατρείου.

Κάλαμος, 29.Χ.72

THE GET-AWAY

They were coming out of the coal mine's shower room. Their feet
  shone.
When the dark's lit up — it's more mysterious. Wet towels
and black spots on the corridor tiles. They didn't know.
Fragmented depictions on the mirrors — horses, forests,
and an iron box left in the mountain's shadow in the afternoon,
as miles away the boat with its empty baskets dwindled away
in a quiet, flaming and crimson sea. It had for oarsman
that handsome, stark-naked fugitive from the insane asylum.

                                        Kálamos, 10/29/72

153

ΧΕΙΜΕΡΙΝΗ ΛΙΑΚΑΔΑ

Μὲ τὴν ὀχτωβριανὴ λιακάδα μέθυσαν οἱ πεταλοῦδες—
χιλιάδες ἄσπρες πεταλοῦδες τρέχοντας στ' ἀγκάθια,
στὶς κίτρινες καλαμποκιές, στὸ ρηχὸ ἀκροθαλάσσι,
κυνηγώντας τὶς γαλανὲς σκιές τους. Νὰ ἐνδώσεις—εἶπε·
νὰ ἐνδώσεις πάλι. Μιὰ ἐλάχιστη εὐγένεια. Ὅλοι θὰ γεράσουν.
Θὰ μαλακώσει κ' ἡ πέτρα στὸ νερό. Ἡ πιὸ λευκὴ πεταλούδα
σταμάτησε στὸ μαῦρο σκοῦφο τοῦ τυφλοῦ. Ἐκεῖνος τὴν πιάνει,
τὴ σπρώχνει ἀνάμεσα στὶς χόρδες μὲ τὰ δυὸ δάχτυλά του
μέσα στὸ στόμιο τῆς κιθάρας·—εἶναι αὐτὴ ποὺ γυρνάει κάθε βράδι
ἔξω ἀπ' τὰ λαϊκὰ ἐστιατόρια τῶν ὁδῶν Σατωβριάνδου καὶ Δώρου.

Κάλαμος, 29.Χ.72

WINTRY SUNSHINE

The butterflies became intoxicated with the October sunshine —
thousands of white butterflies running to the thorns,
to the yellow cornstalks, to the shallow seashore,
chasing their azure shadows. Such abandon — he said —
such abandon again. A slight civility. All will grow old.
Even the stone will soften in the water. The whitest of the
    butterflies
alighted on the black knit cap of the blind man. He caught it,
and with two of his fingers thrust it between the strings
into the mouth of the guitar — it was the one that wandered every
    night
outside the workers' restaurants of Chateaubriand and Dhórou
    Streets.

Kálamos, 10/29/72

155

ΣΤΑΔΙΑΚΗ ΑΠΟΓΥΜΝΩΣΗ

Τὸ ἀλέτρι μπηγμένο στὴ γῆ. Ἕνα μεγάλο καπνισμένο τσουκάλι
ἀνάποδα ριγμένο στὰ ξερὰ χορτάρια. Τὸ σκυλὶ γαυγίζει. Οἱ κόττες
τρέχουν πίσω ἀπ' τὸ συρματόπλεγμα. Στὸ σκοτεινὸ νερὸ τῆς στέρνας
ἐπιπλέει τὸ κόκκινο νάϋλον παιδικὸ αὐτοκίνητο. Κι ὁ κύκνος;
    —ρώτησε.
Ποιὸς κύκνος;—εἶπε ὁ ἄλλος. Δὲν εἶδα κανέναν. Ὁ κύκνος—εἶπε—
ὁ κύκνος.
Ὦ Κύριε, δὲ μὲ ξεγελᾶς, ἐμένα—τουλάχιστον ἐμένα. Ἐγὼ
ξεγέλασα τόσους πεθαμένους,—τοὺς ἔφερα πίσω. Κάτω ἀπ' τὶς πέτρες
βρῆκα στρωμένο τὸ τραπέζι καὶ στὴ μέση, στὴ μεγάλη πιατέλα,
γυμνὸς ὁ κύκνος, Κύριε. Μὲ τὰ λεπτὰ πούπουλά του ἔχω γεμίσει
τὰ δυὸ μαξιλάρια μου. Τὰ πιὸ μεγάλα ἔξη φτερά του, νά τα
ἀγέρωχα στὸν ἀέρα, περασμένα στὸ καπέλο τῆς τρελλῆς.

                                            Κάλαμος, 29.Χ.72

GRADUALLY STRIPPED BARE

A plow thrust into the earth. A large smoke-blackened pot
thrown overturned on the dry grass. A dog barks. Hens
scatter behind the wire netting. In the dark waters of the cistern
a child's red plastic automobile floats. And the swan? — he asked.
What swan? — said the other. I didn't see any. The swan — he
    said — the swan.
O Lord, you cannot deceive me — not me, at least. I've
deceived so many dead — I've brought them back. Under the stones
I found a table spread, and in its middle, on a large plate,
the swan naked, Lord. With its delicate down I've stuffed
my two pillows. And here are its six largest feathers,
arrogant in the wind, passed through the hat of the mad woman.

Kálamos, 10/29/72

157

ΑΤΕΛΕΣΦΟΡΟΙ ΟΡΚΟΙ

Ἀπομεινάρια θερινῶν ἐκδρομῶν πλάϊ στὴ σκάλα, πλαστικὰ φιαλίδια,
νάϋλον σακκοῦλες μὲ μικρὲς ἀράχνες. Ὦ γλυκειὰ ταπεινοσύνη,—
λέει·
μιὰ βάρκα ἀπορριγμένη στὰ χαλίκια, ἐκεῖ ποὺ ἐρχόταν ἡ σιωπηλὴ
γυναίκα
μὲ τὰ μαλλιά της φυσημένα ἀπ᾽ τὴν ἀναπνοὴ τοῦ σώματός της. Κ᾽
ἐμεῖς
δὲν εἴχαμε τίποτα, μήτε τὰ πιὸ συνηθισμένα λόγια. Μόνο ὁ Πέτρος
πήδησε τὸ ὑψωμένο καραβόσκοινο καὶ στάθηκε μπροστά της. Τότε
νύχτωσε μονομιᾶς· σφυρίζαν τὰ κουνούπια· ἀνάψαμε τὴ λάμπα·
κ᾽ ἐκεῖ στὴν πόρτα, ἀσάλευτος μὲς στὴν ταλάντευσή του, ὁ
μεθυσμένος
ἕτοιμος πάλι γιὰ τὸν ἴδιο ἀθετημένον ὅρκο του: νὰ μὴν ξαναμεθύσει.

Ἀθήνα, 30.X.72

158

INEFFECTUAL OATHS

The remnants of summer excursions behind the stairs, plastic
    decanters,
nylon sacks with small spiders. O sweet humility — he says;
a boat thrown up on the shingle, where the silent woman comes
with her hair blown by her body's breath. And we
had nothing, not even the most habitual words. Only Pétros
leaped over the boat's cable and stood before her. Then
night fell abruptly; the mosquitoes whistled; we lit the lamp;
and there by the door, unmoving as he swayed, the drunk
ready once more for his same forsaken vow: not to get drunk again.

Athens, 10/30/72

ΑΥΤΟΦΩΡΟ

Κάθεται στὴν καρέκλα, ἀντίκρυ μου. Γελάει. Τὰ δόντια του
κατάλευκα.
Ὡραῖος, παστρικός· καλοσιδερωμένο τὸ πουκάμισό του. Ὡστόσο, τὸ
ξέρω:
μέσα στὴν τσέπη του ἔχει ἕνα μαντίλι πολὺ λερωμένο. Κοιτάω τὰ
παπούτσια του—
τὄνα εἶναι μαῦρο, τ᾽ ἄλλο καφετί. Πιάνει τὸ βλέμμα μου. Μὴν τὸ
πεῖς ἱκετεύει.
Αὐτὸ μονάχα: μὴν τὸ πεῖς. Βγάζει, μοῦ δίνει τὸ μαντίλι του. Τὸ
παίρνω·
τὸ ξεδιπλώνω· τοῦ τὸ δείχνω· Τὸ βάζω στὴν τσέπη μου. Δὲ θὰ τὸν
μαρτυρήσω.

Ἀθήνα, 30.X.72

160

CAUGHT IN THE ACT

He sits in the chair opposite me. He laughs. His teeth are
  dazzling white.
Handsome, scrubbed clean, his shirt well-ironed. Nevertheless, I
  know:
in his pockets he has a very dirty handkerchief. I look at his
  shoes —
one black, the other brown. He catches my glance. Don't say it —
  he implores me.
This only: don't say it. He takes out his handkerchief, gives it to
  me. I take it,
unfold it, show it to him, then put it in my pocket. I will not testify
  against him.

Athens, 10/30/72

ΑΕΝΑΑ

Ποτήρια, κρεββάτια, μασέλες, ἐπίδεσμοι, κλειδοῦχοι,
φρουροί, φυλακές, κλεφτοφάναρα, καὶ γριές, γριές, γριές,
ἔφυγαν νύχτα μὲ τὸ τραῖνο τῶν 12, ἦρθαν ἄλλες
τὸ ἴδιο γριές, πιὸ γριές, μὲ βαζάκια κρέμες στὶς τσάντες τους·
οἱ καπνοδόχοι κοιτιόνταν στὸν καθρέφτη τοῦ φεγγαριοῦ,
γέρναν ζερβὰ τὸ κεφάλι τους, ἀλλάζαν στάση, δοκιμάζαν
μιὰν ἄλλη ἐποχή, μιὰν ἀνάμνηση, τὸ ἴδιο μαῦρο καπέλο,—
ὁ χάρτης, τὰ κλειδιά, ὁ νυχοκόπτης εἶχαν πέσει στὶς ράγιες,
κ' ἐσὺ μαδοῦσες τὰ δυὸ μόνα σου φτερὰ γιὰ νὰ πετάξεις.

                                            Ἀθήνα, 31.Χ.72

162

PERPETUAL

Water glasses, beds, dentures, bandages, switchmen,
guards, prisons, flashlights, and old women, old women, old women,
departed at night on the 12 o'clock train. Others came,
old women again, older still, with small jars of face cream in their
    purses.
The smokestacks were looking at themselves in the mirror of the
    moon,
tilting their heads to the left, changing position, trying out
another epoch, a recollection, the same black hat —
the map, the keys, the nail clippers had fallen on the tracks,
and you moulting your only two wings that you might fly.

Athens, 10/31/72

ΜΕΣΟΝΥΧΤΙΑ ΚΡΑΥΓΗ

Τὸ ἄγαλμα τῆς εἰσόδου, ὁλόγυμνο, κρατοῦσε τὴ λάμπα. Βγῆκαν κ᾽ οἱ
πέντε ἀπ᾽ τὴν πύλη.
Οἱ δυὸ στραβοπατοῦσαν βάζοντας ἀκόμη τὰ πανωφόρια τους. Οἱ
τοῖχοι
εἶταν ἄσπροι καὶ γκρίζοι. Ὑπῆρχαν σκάλες ἀπὸ μέσα. Στὸ κεφα-
λόσκαλο
στεκόταν ὁ θαλαμηπόλος μὲ τὸ μεγάλο δίσκο. Στὸ πάνω δωμάτιο
ἀκούστηκε ἡ κραυγή· «Σταμάτα. Σταμάτα». Σπάσαν τὰ τζάμια.
Πέταξαν κάτω τὸν καθρέφτη, μετὰ τὴν καρέκλα. «Σταμάτα.
Σταμάτα»—
βαθειὰ κραυγή, γυρνώντας πίσω, ἀντηχώντας στὰ κιούπια τοῦ
ὑπογείου,
μέσα στὸ κούφιο ξύλινο ἄλογο, ὅπου, μέρες τώρα, ὁ κομμωτής
κρυμμένος
ἔφτιαχνε μὲ τὴν ἄγρια κόκκινη χαίτη τὴν περούκα τῆς βασίλισσας.

Ἀθήνα, 31.Χ.72

MIDNIGHT CRY

The naked statue at the entrance held a lamp. All five came out of
   the gate.
Two were wobbling, still putting on their overcoats. The walls
were white and grey. Inside, there were stairs. On the landing
stood the chamberlain with a large tray. On the upper floor
a cry was heard: "Stop! Stop!" They broke the windowpanes,
hurled down the mirror, then the chair. "Stop! Stop!" —
a deep cry, veering back, reverberating in the basement jars,
in the hollow wooden horse where for days now the hairdresser
   hiding there
was making the queen's wig out of its savage red mane.

Athens, 10/31/72

ΑΝΑΠΑΡΑΣΤΑΣΗ

Μὲ διακοπές, μὲ σκόρπια σήματα, συνδέοντας τὸ ἐκκρεμὲς μὲ τὸ
    ποτήρι·—
λέξεις ἀλλιῶς ψιθυρισμένες, ἀνεβαίνοντας ἢ κατεβαίνοντας τὴν ἴδια
    σκάλα·
ἡ κυρία μὲ τὰ μαῦρα, ἡ κυρία μὲ τὰ κίτρινα, ἡ ἄλλη κυρία
γυμνή, μὲ τὶς κόκκινες κάλτσες,—αὐτὴ ποὺ τὴν περίμεναν κάτω
    στὸ δρόμο
τὰ δυὸ αὐτοκίνητα μὲ σβησμένους φανούς. Κυρία μου—εἶπε—
προσέχτε, μὴν ἀνοῖχτε τὴν ὀμπρέλα σας πρὶν βγεῖτε ἀπ' τὴν πόρτα,
ὅταν περνάει εὐθυτενὴς ὁ ὑπηρέτης μὲ τὰ δυὸ χρυσὰ κηροπήγια
κ' οἱ δυὸ ἀντικρυστοὶ καθρέφτες πολλαπλασιάζουν τὰ σταχτοδοχεῖα,
τῆ χάρτινη οὐρά, τὸ γυάλινο κράνος. Ὦ, Κυρία μου, ἡ δημιουργία
ἀπαιτεῖ σπάγγο καλὰ κερωμένο καὶ μεγάλη βελόνα
νὰ ράψεις τῆ λινάτσα πάνω στὸ καλάθι ὅπου ἐντός του ἔχουμε βάλει
τὰ κόκκινα αὐγὰ τυλιγμένα ἕνα - ἕνα σὲ παλιὲς ἐφημερίδες,
μιὰ σοκολάτα, τρία κουτιὰ τσιγάρα, ξυραφάκια, ἁλάτι, μουστάρδα,
καὶ σὲ μιὰν ἄσπρη πετσέτα ἕνα μεγάλο ψωμὶ διάτρητο ἀπ' τὶς
    σφαῖρες.

Ἀθήνα, 31.Χ.72

REPRESENTATION

With interruptions, with scattered signs, uniting the pendulum
   with the water glass —
words we whispered differently on ascending or descending the
   same stairs.
The lady in black, the lady in yellow, the other lady,
naked, with two red stockings — the one they were waiting for
   down in the street,
the two cars with their lights turned off. My Lady — he said —
take care not to open your umbrella before you go out the door,
when the servant, holding himself erect, passes by with the two
   gold candlesticks,
and the two facing mirrors multiply the ash trays,
the paper tail, the glass helmet. Oh, my Lady, creation
requires some string well waxed and a big needle
that you may sew the mat on the basket in which we have placed
red eggs wrapped one by one in old newspapers,
a chocolate bar, three packs of cigarettes, small razor blades, salt,
   mustard,
and in a white napkin a large loaf of bread riddled by bullets.

Athens, 10/31/72

167

ΑΠΟΜΥΖΗΣΗ

Ἡ στάση του ὅλη μιὰ χειρονομία νὰ διώξει τὴ μεγάλη μύγα
ποὺ ἐπίμονα ἐπανέρχονταν στὸ ἴδιο σημεῖο, στὸν κρόταφό του,
στὸ μάγουλό του ἢ στὴ μύτη του. Στὸ τέλος ἀκινήτησε. Ἡ μύγα
ἀκινήτησε κι αὐτὴ στὸ μάγουλό του, τὸν ἀπομυζοῦσε, μεγεθύνονταν.
Στὴ θέση του ἔμεινε μονάχα ἡ μύγα, τυλιγμένη κ' ἐκείνη
στοὺς ἱστοὺς τῆς ἀράχνης, ὅπου σπίθιζαν τὰ σταγονίδια τῆς ὑγρασίας.

'Αθήνα, 1.ΧΙ.72

BLOODLETTING

His behavior was all one gesture to drive away the big fly
that doggedly kept returning to the same spot, to his temple,
to his cheek, to his nose. At last he stood still. The fly
also stood still on his cheek, where it sucked his blood and grew
    larger.
In his place only the fly remained, it too wrapped round
by the spider's cobweb, where droplets of moisture glittered.

Athens, 11/1/72

169

ΑΝΤΙΓΡΑΦΑ ΑΝΤΙΓΡΑΦΩΝ

Μιλοῦσε σὰν ἀδιάφορα· κοιτοῦσε τὰ νύχια του. Ἀπὸ νύχτα σὲ νύχτα
μετακινούμαστε—ἔλεγε,—ἀπ' τὴ μοναξιὰ τοῦ μόνου στὴν ἄλλη
μοναξιὰ τῶν πολλῶν·—καὶ ἡ ἐκλογὴ δὲν εἶναι δική μας. Κρατῶ
τ' ἄδειο παγούρι τοῦ στρατιώτη, τὸ μαστίγιο τοῦ θηριοδαμαστῆ, τὴν
        κάλτσα
μαύρη καὶ τρύπια τῆς Κασσάνδρας, τὰ ψεύτικα γένεια τοῦ
        Ἀγαμέμνονα·
ρίχνω τὸ πανωφόρι στὸ κεφάλι μου· σκοτεινιάζω· ἀνασαίνω
πολὺ σιγὰ μὴ καὶ μ' ἀκούσουν οἱ τσέπες μου· σὲ λίγο μισανοίγω
μιὰ χαραμάδα στὰ δυὸ φύλλα τοῦ πανωφοριοῦ μου· συλλαμβάνω
μὲς στὸν καθρέφτη τόνα μου μάτι· πιάνω μυστικὴ φιλία μαζί του·
ζεσταίνομαι· πετῶ τὰ ροῦχα μου· ἀπομένω θεόγυμνος
πλάϊ στὸ γυμνὸ ἄγαλμά μου. Μπαίνουν ξάφνου οἱ τρεῖς γυναῖκες
μὲ τὰ λαχανικά τους μὲς σὲ κίτρινα νάϋλον δίχτυα. Ἐγὼ
δὲν ἔχω τίποτ' ἄλλο πιὰ νὰ κάνω ἀπ' τὸ νὰ μείνω ἀδέξια ἀσάλευτος
ὑποκρινόμενος ὅσο μπορῶ καλύτερα τὸ ἄγαλμα τοῦ ἀγάλματός μου.

                                              Ἀθήνα, 1.XI.72

IMITATION OF AN IMITATION

He spoke with a studied indifference, gazing at his fingernails.
  Night after night — he said —
we are transferred from the loneliness of one person to that other
  loneliness
of the many — and the choice is not ours. I hold
the soldier's empty canteen, the animal tamer's whip, Cassandra's
black stocking full of holes, Agamemnon's false beard;
I throw the overcoat over my head, I darken, breathe
very quietly so that my pockets won't hear me; in a little while
I half open a crack in the two folds of my overcoat, catch sight
of one of my eyes in the mirror, begin a secret friendship with it,
grow heated, cast off my clothing, and remain stark naked
beside my naked statue. Suddenly three women come in
with their vegetables in three nylon net bags. I now
have nothing more to do than to remain clumsily motionless,
playing the part as well as I can of my statue's statue.

Athens, 11/1/72

ΑΝΤΙΚΡΥΣΤΑ

Αὐτὸς ποὺ εἶδε τὰ δέντρα, τὰ βουνά, τὰ σύννεφα, τὴ δόξα τῶν
    χρωμάτων,
αὐτὸς ποὺ ἀκούμπησε τ᾽ αὐτί του στὸ καυτὸ χῶμα ἀκούγοντας τὸν
    καλπασμὸ τῶν ἀλόγων,
τὰ βήματα τῶν διαδηλωτῶν καὶ τὰ καρότσια τῶν ἀνάπηρων πολέμου,
ὁ ἴδιος αὐτὸς ποὺ πότισε στὴ βρύση ντάλα μεσημέρι τὶς δώδεκα
    ἀγελάδες
ξυπόλυτος μὲ τὰ πλατάνια καὶ τὶς σημαῖες· —δὲν μπορῶ νὰ τὸν
    βλέπω
ἔτσι κατάχαμα στὸ πάτωμα, μὲ τὰ μεγάλα τρύπια του παπούτσια,
    νὰ κυλάει
μὲ τὄνα του δάχτυλο, διαιρώντας, πολλαπλασιάζοντας, μετρώντας
τὰ σταγονίδια τοῦ ὑδραργύρου ἀπὸ κεῖνο τὸ σπασμένο θερμόμετρο
ποὔπεσε, πόσα χρόνια πρίν, ἀπ᾽ τὴ μασχάλη τῆς Ἰοκάστης.

Ἀθήνα, 1.XI.72

FACE TO FACE

He who saw the trees, the mountains, the clouds, the glory of the
   colors,
who set his ear to the hot earth, listening to the galloping of
   horses,
to the tread of the demonstrators and the carts of disabled
   veterans;
the same who watered the twelve cows at the spring on the drop
   of noon,
barefooted by the plane trees and the flags — I cannot bear to
   look at him
like this, sprawled on the floor, with his large shoes full of holes,
dividing, multiplying, counting with one finger
the beads of mercury from the broken thermometer
that fell, so many years ago, from Jocasta's armpit.

                                    Athens, 11/1/72

173

ΔΙΟΓΚΩΜΕΝΑ ΕΜΠΟΔΙΑ

Χτυπήματα σφυριῶν ὁλημερὶς κάτω ἀπ' τὸ λόφο. Ἐκεῖ
ἀνηφορίζουν πρὸς τὸ βράδι οἱ δυὸ τελωνοφύλακες
βουβοί, σκυθρωποί, ἔχοντας μὲς στὴν τσέπη τους
ἀδιάβαστη ἀκόμα τὴν πρωϊνὴ ἐφημερίδα
πρόχειρα διπλωμένη. Κ' ἐσὺ ποὺ κοιτᾶς
τὴ θάλασσα, τὸ σκύλο, τὶς σκοινένιες σκάλες
δὲν μπορεῖς πιὰ νὰ καταλάβεις οὔτε νὰ δικαιολογήσεις
τοὺς χτύπους τῶν σφυριῶν, γιατὶ στὶς τσέπες τῶν τελωνοφυλάκων,
σ' ἐκείνη τὴν ἐφημερίδα τους ποὺ δὲ διαβάσαν, εἶναι τυπωμένη
μιὰ νεανικὴ φωτογραφία σου, καὶ τὰ ρουθούνια σου ἔχουν φράξει
ἀπὸ μάλλινα χνούδια, ἀπὸ σισάμι, ἀπὸ τρίμματα καπνοῦ,
καὶ μιὰ ὀδοντογλυφίδα κάθε τόσο σοῦ τρυπάει τὸ πηγούνι.

Ἀθήνα, 2.ΧΙ.72

INFLATED OBSTACLES

Hammer blows all day long under the hill. There,
ascending toward evening, were the two customs officials,
silent, somber, the morning paper carelessly folded,
still unread, in their pockets. And you who gaze
at the sea, the dog, the rope ladders,
can no longer understand or justify
the hammer blows, because in the pockets of the customs officials,
in that paper of theirs which they have not read, a youthful
picture of you is printed, and your nostrils are clogged
with woolen fluff, sesame seed, tobacco shreds,
and a toothpick which ever so often pricks your chin.

Athens, 11/2/72

175

Ο ΧΩΜΑΤΕΝΙΟΣ ΕΦΗΒΟΣ

Όμορφα πόδια γυμνά, λασπωμένα ὣς ἀπάνω στὰ γόνατα.
Σίγουρα, θἄχε ποτίσει τὸ περβόλι. Ἡ λάσπη,—ἔλεγε—ἡ λάσπη·
τὸ ζυμωμένο χῶμα, τὸ πιάνω μὲ τὰ χέρια μου, νά το,
τὸ σφίγγω μὲς στὶς φοῦχτες μου, κολλάει στὰ δάχτυλά μου,
δὲ φτιάχνω σταμνιὰ μήτε λυχνάρια μήτε γλάστρες·
τὶς πατάτες τὶς μπήγω στὴ γῆς. Ἀγναντεύω μακριὰ τὰ χαράκια
ἀπ' τοὺς τροχοὺς τῆς βοϊδάμαξας, ὣς τὸ βάθος τοῦ δρόμου,
βαθιὰ χαράκια στὴ λάσπη, κρουστά, σὰν τὰ ποδάρια
τοῦ γεωργοῦ ποὺ πλάγιασε ἀνάσκελα κι ἀποκοιμήθηκε ἀμέσως
χωρὶς νὰ ροχαλίζει. Ἀπὸ τὴ μιὰ καὶ τὴν ἄλλη μεριὰ
κάθονται δυὸ σειρὲς σπουργίτια καὶ τσιμπολογᾶνε σπόρους.
Ἀνάμεσά τους εἶναι ἕνα καλάθι σκεπασμένο μὲ πετσέτα.
Αὐτὸ τὸ καλάθι τὸ παίρνω τὸ βράδι καὶ γυρνάω στὸ πατρικό μου.

Ἀθήνα, 3.XI.72

176

THE EARTHEN ADOLESCENT

Beautiful naked feet, muddy up to the knees.
Surely, he must have watered the garden. The mud — he'd say —
    the mud;
the kneaded earth, I grasp it in my hands, here it is,
I squeeze it in my fists, it sticks to my fingers,
I do not make jugs or lanterns or flower pots.
I thrust potatoes into the earth. In the distance I can make out
the wheel tracks of the oxcart far down the road,
deep tracks in the mud, crusty, like the big feet
of the farmer who lay down on his back and fell asleep at once
without snoring. On one side and the other. On either side
sparrows are sitting in two rows and nibbling at seeds.
Between them is a basket covered with a napkin.
I take this basket every morning and return to my paternal home.

Athens, 11/3/72

177

ΕΙΚΟΝΟΓΡΑΦΟΙ

Κλεπταποδόχος, λέει, βυζαντινῶν εἰκόνων, αὐτὸς ὁ ὑπερόπτης,
αὐτὸς ποὺ σήκωσε, τὴν τελευταία στιγμή, τὸ δάχτυλό του
μπροστὰ στοὺς μοναχοὺς καὶ στὸν ἀρχιερέα, καταγγέλλοντας
τοὺς τρεῖς φημισμένους ἁγιογράφους, δείχνοντας σ' ὅλους
μιὰ - μιὰ τὶς εἰκόνες—σὲ καμμιὰ ἀπ' τὶς μορφὲς τῶν ἁγίων
δὲν ὑπῆρχαν αὐτιά·—καταγγέλλοντας βέβαια καὶ μᾶς
ποὺ ποτέ μας δὲν τόχαμε προσέξει, (ἴσως ἡ λάμψη
τῶν φωτοστέφανων μᾶς θάμπωνε τὰ μάτια). Λίγο ἀργότερα
κατασκευάζαμε μὲ ξέχωρη ἐπιμέλεια τ' αὐτιὰ τῶν ἁγίων
καταργώντας λίγο - λίγο τὰ φωτοστέφανα. Καὶ τώρα,
τὴν ὥρα τῆς δουλειᾶς, ψαύαμε μὲ τ' ἀριστερό μας χέρι
τὶς ἄκρες τῶν αὐτιῶν μας ἀργά, μυστικά, ὑποψιασμένοι
μήπως καὶ τούτη τὴ φορὰ δὲν εἴχαμε ἀκούσει καλά.

'Αθήνα, 3.XI.72

ICONOGRAPHERS

A receiver of stolen goods, he said, of Byzantine icons, this
   presumptuous person,
this man who at the last minute raised his finger
before the monks and the high priest and accused
the three renowned hagiographers, showing the icons
to all, one by one — there was not a single ear
on any of the saints' faces — accusing us as well, of course,
for not having ever observed this (perhaps the brilliance
of the haloes had dazzled our eyes). A little later
we constructed the saints' ears with particular diligence,
eradicating the haloes little by little. And now,
while we are working, we feel the edges of our own ears
with our left hands, slowly, secretly, suspecting
that even this time perhaps we had not heard correctly.

Athens, 11/3/72

179

ΕΠΑΓΡΥΠΝΗΣΗ

Μέσα στὸν ὕπνο παρακολουθεῖ τὸν ὕπνο του, σὲ μιὰ βραδύτητα
ποὺ καταργεῖ τὸ χρόνο. Δοκιμάζει πάλι. Ἀνοίγει τὸ βῆμα·
περπατάει στὸν ἀέρα·—ἕνας φαρδὺς διασκελισμὸς διαρκείας·
ἀκινητεῖ στὴν πιὸ στέρεη ἐλαφρότητα. Κάτω ἀπ' τὰ σκέλη του
διέρχονται μεγάλα ἀργόπορα τρίγωνα, μόλις ἐγγίζοντας
τοὺς μηροὺς καὶ τὶς κνῆμες του· προχωροῦν μαλακὰ πρὸς τὰ πίσω
σὰν ἀνοιξιάτικα σύννεφα. Στὴν κορυφὴ τοῦ ἑνὸς τριγώνου
εἶναι τὰ γάντια του. Στὴν κορυφὴ τοῦ δευτέρου, τὸ καπέλο του.
Στὴν κορυφὴ τοῦ τρίτου ἕνα γαλάζιο ποτήρι, ποὺ δὲν τὄχε.
Ὅταν ξυπνήσει, μ' αὐτὸ θὰ πιεῖ νερὸ καὶ μετὰ θὰ τὸ κρύψει
στὸ ντουλάπι τοῦ τοίχου μαζὶ μὲ τὴν τανάλια καὶ τὸ ξυπνητήρι.

Μπορεῖ, λοιπόν, νὰ σταθεῖ στὸν ἀέρα, νὰ κυβερνήσει τὴ μοίρα;

Ἀθήνα, 4.XI.72

180

VIGILANCE

In his sleep he observes his sleep with a sluggishness
that abolishes time. He tries again. He takes greater strides,
walks on air — a wide stride of long duration;
he remains motionless on the firmest weightlessness. Under his legs
cross large slow-moving triangles, barely touching
his thigh and his shanks; they continue smoothly backward
like spring clouds. On the tip of one triangle
are his gloves. On the tip of the second, his hat.
On the tip of the third, a blue water glass he never had.
When he wakes up, he'll drink water from this and then hide it
in the wall cupboard together with the pliers and the alarm-clock.

Can he, therefore, stand on air, govern his fate?

Athens, 11/4/72

181

ΚΑΡΤΕΡΙΚΗ ΓΝΩΣΗ

Λευτέρη, τὸ ψωμὶ εἶναι ξερό, τὸ νερὸ ζεσταμένο. Στάσου.
Μὴν τὸ κουρντίσεις τὸ ρολόϊ. Στὴ σωστὴ του ὥρα σταμάτησε. Ἔξω
εἶναι ἕνα δέντρο,—τὸ βλέπω—ἔτσι ντυμένο μ' ἐλάχιστα φύλλα—
ἡ διαφάνειά τους εἶναι τὸ τέλος τους. Ὡστόσο ἕνα διάφανο τέλος
ποτὲ δὲν εἶναι τέλος. Γι' αὐτὸ καὶ δὲ σοῦ κρύβω τίποτα. Στὸ τραπέζι,
πλάϊ στὰ τσιγάρα, πλάϊ στὴ μικρὴ πεθαμένη χελώνα,
ἔχω ἀφημένα σὲ παράταξη, κατὰ μεγέθη, τὰ κλειδιά μου.

Ἀθήνα, 4.ΧΙ.72

182

PATIENT KNOWLEDGE

Leftéris, the bread is dry, the water has grown warm. Wait.
Don't wind the clock. It stopped on its precise hour. Outside
is a tree — I see it — dressed with very few leaves —
their transparency is their end. Nevertheless, a transparent end
is never an end. This is why I'm not hiding anything from you.
On the table, beside the cigarettes, beside the small dead turtle,
I've left my keys, arranged in order according to their size.

Athens, 11/4/72

ΕΝΔΕΙΞΕΙΣ

Τὸ φῶς διαθλᾶται σὲ κανονικὰ διαστήματα στὸν τοῖχο
ὅπως ἡ καρωτίδα τῆς ἄρρωστης γυναίκας. Ὡστόσο, στὸν ἀέρα
ἐπιπλέει ἡ ἀόριστη αἴσθηση θερμή, κάποιου ἀντικειμένου
πολὺ στερεοῦ, πολὺ πράσινου, σχεδὸν τετράγωνου, κρυμμένου
κάτω ἀπ' τὸ κρεββάτι ἐκστρατείας μὲ τὰ παπούτσια τοῦ μοιχοῦ.
Ἴσως γι' αὐτὸ κοιτάζουμε ἔντονα τὴ φωτισμένη βιτρίνα
ὁλότελα κίτρινη μὲ τὰ δυὸ μαῦρα λιοντάρια. Κ' ἴσως γι' αὐτὸ
τὰ στόματα στὶς προσωπίδες μένουν πάντοτε ὁλάνοιχτα
γιὰ νὰ μιλάει μὲ βαθύτερη εἰλικρίνεια ἀπὸ μέσα τους ὁ ἄλλος.

Ἀθήνα, 4.ΧΙ.72

INDICATIONS

The light is refracted at regular intervals on the wall
like the carotid artery of the sick woman. Nevertheless, the vague
warm sensation of some object floats in the air,
very firm, very green, almost square, hidden
under the army camp bed with the shoes of the adulterer.
Perhaps this is why we look so intensely in a lit shop window
completely yellow with two black lions. Perhaps this is why
the mouths of the masks always gape open,
that the other within them may speak with greater candor.

Athens, 11/4/72

ΦΘΙΝΟΠΩΡΙΝΗ ΑΝΤΑΠΟΚΡΙΣΗ

Τὶς ξέρεις κεῖνες τὶς ἐπαύλεις πλάϊ στὴ θάλασσα ἢ πάνω στοὺς
    λόφους
κατάκλειστες στὰ τέλη τοῦ φθινόπωρου, τὸ ἀπόγευμα σὰν ψιχαλίζει
ἢ τὰ πρωϊνὰ σὲ μιὰν ἄξαφνη λιακάδα, πιότερο ἀκόμη κλεισμένες
ἀπ᾽ τὶς ἀραιές, ὀξεῖες φωνὲς τῶν σπουργιτιῶν στὸν κοντινὸ ἐλαιώνα
κι ἀπ᾽ τὶς νεκρώσιμες ντουφεκιὲς τῶν κυνηγῶν. Στὶς αὐλές τους
πέφτουν μὲ κούφιο θόρυβο τ᾽ ἀγριάπιδα λιθοβολώντας
τὸ ἀόρατο ποὺ κατακάθησε καὶ πιὰ δὲ δίνει στόχο. Κ᾽ ἡ φωνή:
«Ἀγλαΐα, Ἀγλαΐα», μπουκωμένη μὲ μαῦρο μπαμπάκι. Στὶς κάμαρες
σωριάζονται ἔντομα νεκρά, πεταλοῦδες τῆς νύχτας, ἀράχνες,
στεγνὰ φτερά, κλωστές, τρίμματα γύψου. Τὸ ἄσκοπο—εἶπε ὁ
    Παῦλος—
εἰσδύει μαζὶ μὲ τὴν κρυφίνοη ὑγρασία μέσα στοὺς τοίχους,
μέσα στὰ πιὸ προφυλαγμένα μπαοῦλα, καπελιέρες, ντουλάπες,
ἐκεῖ ποὺ φύλαγαν τὰ παλιὰ νυφικά, τὰ χαλασμένα ρολόγια. Κι
    ἄξαφνα
ἀκούστηκε στὸ κλειδωμένο κίτρινο σπίτι μιὰ σκούπα ἠλεκτρικὴ
ἴσως γιὰ νὰ καλύψει τὶς πυκνὲς πιστολιὲς στὸ διπλανὸ χωράφι
ἐκεῖ ποὺ συνεχίζαν τὶς χαριστικὲς βολὲς στὸ πλαγιασμένο ὁλόγυμνο
    σῶμα.

Κάλαμος, 5.ΧΙ.72

AUTUMNAL CORRESPONDENCE

You know those villas beside the sea or on hilltops,
firmly shut at the end of autumn, in the afternoon when it's
    drizzling,
or in the mornings in a burst of sunlight, still more firmly shut
by the infrequent shrill sounds of sparrows in the olive trees nearby,
and by the deadly gunblasts of the hunters. In their courtyards
the wild pears fall with a muffled sound, stoning
the invisible which has subsided and is no longer a target. And the
    voice:
"Aghlaía, Aghlaía," stuffed with black cotton. In the rooms
dead insects fall in heaps, night butterflies, spiders,
dry feathers, strings, scraps of plaster. Whatever is aimless —
    said Pétros —
penetrates together with insiduous humidity into the walls,
into the most protected trunks, hat boxes, closets
where they've kept old wedding dresses, broken clocks. And
    suddenly
an electric sweeper was heard in the locked yellow house,
perhaps to cover up the repeated pistol shots in the adjacent field
where they continued the final strokes of mercy on the sprawled
    naked body.

Kálamos, 11/5/72

187

ΤΟ «ΑΠΟΓΕΥΜΑ»

«Θὰ ξανάρθω τὸ ἀπόγευμα», ψιθύρισε, παρ᾽ ὅτι κανένας
δὲν εἶταν γύρω του. Κ᾽ ἡ λέξη ἀ π ό γ ε υ μ α ἔμεινε στὸν ἀέρα
ὅπως ὁ ἀεροπόρος ποὺ τὸν βρήκαμε (στ᾽ ἀλήθεια, ἕνα ἀπόγευμα)
κρεμασμένον ψηλὰ στὸ φανοστάτη. Οἱ δώδεκα ναῦτες
εἶχαν σαρώσει τὰ γύρω σοκάκια χωρὶς νὰ βροῦν γυναῖκες.
Τότε ξεμάκρυνε ὁ Βαγγέλης νὰ οὐρήσει πίσω ἀπ᾽ τὴ μάντρα.
Ἔσκισε μιὰ φωτογραφία· τὴ σκόρπισε στὸν ἀέρα. Ἕνα κομμάτι,
ἴσως τὸ κυριότερο, κόλλησε στὰ χείλη μου. Τόκρυψα.

Κάλαμος, 5.ΧΙ.72

188

THE "AFTERNOON"

"I'll return in the afternoon," he whispered, although there was
    no one
around him. The word *afternoon* remained in the air
like an aviator found (truly, one afternoon)
hanging high up on the lamppost. The twelve sailors
had scoured the nearby back streets in vain for women.
Then Vangélis went further off to urinate behind the wall.
He tore up a photograph and scattered it in the air. A piece,
perhaps the most important one, stuck to my lips. I hid it.

Kálamos, 11/5/72

189

ΣΤΟΝ ΠΡΩΤΟ ΚΗΠΟ

Καθόταν στὸ παγκάκι, κάτω ἀπ' τὰ δέντρα. Ἕνα μῆλο
τὴ χτύπησε στὸν ὦμο,—ἴσως καὶ νᾶταν τὸ φεγγάρι. Αὐτὴ
τὸ πῆρε καὶ τὸ δάγκωσε ἔτσι μὲ τὸ φλούδι. Ἄχ, ἀκατόρθωτο—
    εἶπε—
κρυμμένο στὰ νύχια μας, στὸν ἀέρα κι ἀκόμη πιὸ μέσα
μὲ τὶς ἀράχνες, μὲ τὶς σάπιες ρίζες, μὲ τ' ἄσπρα σκουλήκια
καὶ μὲ τὴ σιδερένια πόρπη ἀπ' τὴ ζώνη τοῦ νεκροῦ πολεμιστῆ.

Ἀθήνα, 6.XI.72

IN THE FIRST GARDEN

She was sitting on the small bench under the trees. An apple
hit her on the shoulder — it might even have been the moon. She
took it and bit into it, rind and all. Ah, impossible — she said —
it's hidden in our nails, in the air, and still further in
with the spiders, with rotted roots, with white worms
and with the iron buckle from the belt of the dead warrior.

Athens, 11/6/72

191

ΛΥΤΡΑ

Ἔκοψε στὴ λαμαρίνα ἕναν κύκνο. Τὴν ἔβαψε
μ' ἄσπρη λαδομπογιά. Τὴν ἔρριξε στὴ λίμνη. Βούλιαξε.
Βούτηξε τότε κ' ἔβγαλε τὸ ψάρι. Οἱ ἄλλοι τὸν κοίταζαν. Ἔτρεμε.
Τὰ ροῦχα του κολλημένα στὸ σῶμα του σὰν πήλινο πρόπλασμα
σκεπασμένο μὲ βρεγμένες λινάτσες. Τὸ ἴδιο βράδι
εἶχε δυὸ κύκνους καὶ πολὺ πυρετό. Ὅταν τοῦ βγάλαν τὶς λινάτσες
εἶταν μονάχα μιὰ καρέκλα καὶ πάνω της τὸ ρολόϊ τοῦ χεριοῦ του.

Ἀθήνα, 6.XI.72

LITER

He cut a swan out of a sheet of tin, painted it white
in oils, then threw it into the lake. It sank.
He plunged in then and brought out a fish. The others watched him.
He was shivering, his clothes stuck to his body like a clay model
covered with a wet sackcloth. That same evening
he had two swans and a high fever. When they took off the
   sackcloth,
they found a chair only with his wrist watch on it.

Athens, 11/6/72

193

ΠΑΝΤΟΥ ΟΙ ΜΑΡΤΥΡΕΣ

Τὸ ἄγαλμα δὲν ἔχει προτιμήσεις οὔτε κἂν ἀντιρρήσεις.
Δὲν κρίνει τὴ χειρονομία σου. Ὁλόγυμνο, ἀδιάφορο
μέσα στὴν ἀλαζονική του ὑποταγή. Δὲν μπορεῖς
νὰ εἰσδύσεις μὲς στὴν πέτρα. Ἀπομένεις
ἔξω ἀπ' τὸ ἄγαλμα. Βγάζεις ἀπ' τὸ λαιμό σου τὸ σκοινὶ
καὶ τὸ περνᾶς προσεχτικὰ στὸ λαιμό του. Πιὸ πέρα,
ἀνάμεσα στ' ἀγάλματα ἢ μέσα στ' ἀγάλματα, κάποιος
σὲ παρακολουθεῖ—ὁ φύλακας ἴσως τοῦ μουσείου, ἴσως
ὁ γιὸς τοῦ ξυλουργοῦ ἢ ὁ θάνατός σου. Δὲν προφταίνεις.
Τὸ σπέρμα σου τινάζεται στὶς λευκές, ἀπαστράπτουσες πλάκες.

Ἀθήνα, 11.XI.72

WITNESSES EVERYWHERE

The statue has no preferences, not even any objections.
It doesn't judge your gesture. Completely naked, unconcerned
in its arrogant submission. You cannot
penetrate into the stone. You remain
outside the statue. You take off the rope from your neck
and pass it carefully around its neck. A little further off,
between the statues or amid the statues, someone
is watching you, the museum guard, perhaps
the carpenter's son, or your death. You're not in time.
Your sperm spurts on the white, glistening tiles.

Athens, 11/11/72

ΣΥΜΒΟΛΙΚΑ

Ὅ,τι εἶναι, εἶναι,—λέει. Κοιτάει ἀπ᾽ τὸ παράθυρο γαλήνια.
Δὲν ὠφελεῖ νὰ τ᾽ ἀρνηθεῖς. Ὁ ἀνθοπώλης ραντίζει τὰ λουλούδια.
Ὁ ἀγέρας ἀγκαλιάζει τὸ ἥσυχο δέντρο μὲ τὰ δυό του χέρια.
Ἔρχεται ἡ γυναίκα. Πρὶν μιλήσει, κοιτάει στὸν καθρέφτη.
Ἐσὺ ποὺ λὲς «ὄνειρο μόνο», ψέματα λές. Ξέρω τὸ ἐμπόδιο.
Ἔβαψα τὰ χαρτόνια κόκκινα. Τ᾽ ἅπλωσα στὸ πάτωμα.
Νὰ ζωγραφίσω μὲ κόκκινο στὸ κόκκινο; Τὸ καράβι
τὅφτιαξα μαῦρο, καὶ τὰ δυὸ κατάρτια. Τοῦ πηγαίνει. Μαύρους
τοὺς ὀχτὼ γυμνοὺς κωπηλάτες. Τὴ γοργόνα τῆς πλώρης
μαύρη κι αὐτὴν μὲ δυὸ κόκκινες τρύπες στὰ στήθη.
Ἄγκυρα δὲ ζωγράφισα,—ὄχι ποὺ τὸ ξέχασα. Στὴ θέση της
ἔβαλα τὸ πραγματικὸ ψαλίδι ἐντελῶς στομωμένο
ἀπ᾽ τὰ νύχια τῶν πέντε λιονταριῶν ποὺ εἶχα κόψει.

Ἀθήνα, 11.ΧΙ.72

SYMBOLICAL

Whatever is, is — he says. He gazes serenely out the window.
It's no use denying it. The florist is spraying the flowers.
The wind embraces the quiet tree with both its hands.
The woman is coming. Before speaking, she looks into the mirror.
You who say "only a dream" are lying. I know the obstacle.
I painted the carnations red. I spread them out on the floor.
Shall I draw with red on red? The ship
I made black, and the two masts. The color suits it. Black
also the eight naked oarsmen. The mermaid on the prow
also black with two red holes on each breast.
I didn't draw an anchor — not that I forgot. In its place
I placed the real scissors, completely blunted
by the claws of the five lions I had trimmed.

Athens, 11/11/72

ΑΚΑΘΟΡΙΣΤΟ ΣΧΕΔΙΟ

Ὄμορφο χρῶμα διαλεγμένο ἀπ᾽ τὴν πιὸ μακρινὴ ὀροσειρά.
Ἡ μνήμη τοῦ ἔρωτα κ᾽ ἡ ἀναμονή του. Ὄχι, ὄχι,—εἶπε ὁ ἄλλος.
Ἄφησε τὴν καρέκλα του στὸν ἴσκιο τοῦ δέντρου. Δὲν κάθησε.
Μικρὰ πουλιά, πολὺ μικρὰ σὰν τὰ νύχια του, περπατοῦσαν
στὸ νοτισμένο χορτάρι. Ἐσὺ δὲν ἤξερες πιὰ τί νὰ κάνεις.
Τόνιωθες ποὺ χρωστοῦσες τὰ ροῦχα σου, τὰ ὑπάρχοντά σου,
ἐσώρρουχα, κάλτσες, παπούτσια, στὸ μέλλον. Δὲν τοῦ τὅπες.
Προχώρησες μόνος πρὸς τὴ θάλασσα ἀνασφάλιστος
μὲ τὸ ἴδιο βάρος στὴ μασκάλη σου ἀπ᾽ τὴν ἀπουσία τῆς σκάλας.
Κ᾽ ἐκεῖνα τὰ μικρὰ πουλιὰ νὰ σοῦ κόβουν ἕνα - ἕνα τὰ κουμπιά σου.

Κάλαμος, 12.XI.72

VAGUE DESIGN

Beautiful color selected from the farthest mountain ridge.
The remembrance of love and its expectation. No, no — said the
   other.
He left his chair under the tree's shade. He didn't sit down.
Small birds, very small, like his fingernails, were walking
on the damp grass. You no longer knew what to do.
You felt you owed your clothes, your possessions,
underwear, socks, shoes, to the future. You didn't tell him,
but went on by yourself toward the sea, insecure,
with the same weight under your armpit of the ladder's absence.
And those small birds that cut off your buttons one by one.

Kálamos, 11/12/72

199

ΕΡΩΤΗΜΑΤΙΚΟ ΣΥΜΠΕΡΑΣΜΑ

Τὰ πράγματα φτηναίνουν. Τὰ μαλλιὰ ἀποχρωματίζονται, ἀραιώνουν.
Μεγάλες σκοτεινὲς κηλίδες διαστίζουν τὰ χέρια. Οἱ τρεῖς νάνοι
πετᾶνε τὰ σπασμένα τζάμια πίσω ἀπ' τὸ μαντρότοιχο. Ἡ γριὰ
ἔρχεται ξεροβήχοντας. Κοντοστέκει στὴν πόρτα. Νὰ μπῶ;—λέει.
Ἀφήνει στὸ κρεββάτι δυὸ μεγάλα αὐγά. Φεύγει πάλι. Τότε
ἀκούγεται τὸ ξύλινο πόδι τοῦ ὄμορφου ἀνάπηρου πάνω στὴ σκάλα.
Αὐτό, λοιπόν, ποὺ λέμε ἀπώλεια, μήπως εἶναι συμπλήρωμα;

Κάλαμος, 12.ΧΙ.72

QUESTIONING CONCLUSION

Things cheapen. The hair loses its color, thins out. Large dark
    spots dot the hands. The three dwarfs
throw the broken windowpane behind the courtyard wall. The old
    woman
comes, racked with a dry cough. She hesitates by the door. Shall I
    come in? — she says.
On the bed she leaves two large eggs. She goes away. Then
the wooden leg of the handsome invalid is heard on the stairs.
This, then, which we call a loss — is it perhaps something added?

Kálamos, 11/12/72

201

ΣΚΟΤΕΙΝΟ ΜΑΓΑΖΙ

Τὸ μαγαζὶ εἶταν σκοτεινό. Δυὸ φαντάροι
ἀγόραζαν τσιγάρα. Στὴ δεξιὰ γωνιά, στὸ βάθος,
εἶταν ἡ ζυγαριά. Μιὰ σκιώδης γυναίκα
ἀνέβηκε νὰ ζυγιστεῖ. Οἱ φαντάροι κοιτοῦσαν.
Ὁ δείκτης δὲ μετακινήθηκε. Ἴσως ἡ ζυγαριὰ
νἄχε χαλάσει ἢ πιθανὸν νὰ μὴ φαίνονταν
οἱ ἀριθμοὶ στὸ σκοτάδι. Τὸ πιθανότερο ἀπ᾽ ὅλα
νὰ μὴν εἶχε διόλου βάρος ἡ γυναίκα. Ὡστόσο,
καθὼς ὕψωσε ἀναίτια τὸ ἕνα της χέρι,
ἔπεσαν δυὸ μποτίλιες μπύρα ἀπ᾽ τὸ ράφι,
ἔσπασαν στὰ πλακάκια καὶ τῆς ἔβρεξαν τὰ πόδια.

Κάλαμος, 12.XI.72

THE DARK SHOP

The shop was dark. Two soldiers
were buying cigarettes. In the right corner, in the back,
stood a weighing machine. A shadowy woman
got on the machine to weigh herself. The soldiers watched.
The pointer did not move. Perhaps the weighing machine
was out of order or, probably, the numbers
could not be seen in the dark. It was most likely, however,
that the woman weighed nothing at all. Nevertheless,
as she was innocently raising one of her hands,
two bottles of beer fell from the shelf,
broke on the tiles, and wet her feet.

Kálamos, 11/12/72

203

ΟΧΙ ΠΙΑ

Στὸ πάτωμα πέντε στεφάνια ἀπὸ παλιὰ βαρέλια. Ἐκεῖνος
τὰ σκέπασε μ' ἐφημερίδες, σύρματα, κομμάτια σπάγγους,
ἴσως νὰ προστατέψει τὴ θνητότητά του (κι ἀπὸ ποιὰν ἐπίθεση;)
τῆς μεγαλύτερης—εἶπε—ἀναμονῆς. Καὶ κράτησε στὰ χείλη
τὶς ὑπόλοιπες πρόκες σφιχτά, βρίσκοντας ἕνα πρόσχημα
νὰ μὴν ἀπαντήσει στὴ δεύτερη ἐρώτηση, νὰ μὴν ἀρθρώσει
τὸν ἴδιον ὅρκο ποὺ οὔτε τώρα θὰ μποροῦσε νὰ κρατήσει.

Ἀθήνα, 13.ΧΙ.72

NO LONGER

On the floor were five hoops from old barrels. He
covered them up with newspapers, wire, pieces of string,
perhaps to protect his mortality (and from what attack?).
From the greatest of all — he said — expectation. And he held
the rest of the nails tightly between his lips, finding an excuse
not to answer the second question, not to utter
the same oath he would never now be able to keep.

Athens, 11/13/72

ΔΙΣΤΑΓΜΟΣ

Τὰ γυμνὰ χέρια, τὸ ἄνοιγμα στὸ λαιμό, τὰ ὡραῖα μαλλιὰ
πεσμένα στὸ στόμα. Τί προετοιμάζεται πάλι σὲ τοῦτο τὸ σπίτι,
ὅταν ὑψώνεται ἄξαφνα σὰν ἄλογο στὰ δυό του πόδια τὸ κρεββάτι
τινάζοντας στὸ πάτωμα σεντόνια, μαξιλάρια, τὴν κόκκινη κουβέρτα,
δείχνοντας κάτω του ἕνα ἄπλυτο ποτήρι, τοῦφες χνούδια, σπίρτα
καὶ δυὸ γεροντικά, δυστυχισμένα παπούτσια, φρεσκοβερνικωμένα;

’Αθήνα, 13.ΧΙ.72

206

HESITATION

The naked hands, the opening of the throat, the beautiful hair
fallen to the mouth. What is being prepared in this house again
when like a horse on its two hind feet the bed suddenly rears up,
tossing on the floor bedsheets, pillows, the red blanket,
revealing under it a dirty water glass, bits of fluff, matches,
and two aged, miserable shoes, freshly polished?

Athens, 11/13/72

207

Η ΕΛΞΗ ΤΗΣ ΓΗΣ

Ἕνα φεγγάρι κολλημένο στὰ τζάμια σὰ σφραγισμένο γραμματόσημο
σὲ ἀνεπίδοτο γράμμα. Τὰ κλειστὰ ἐπιπλοποιεῖα ὅλο τραπέζια,
πολυθρόνες, καθρέφτες. Ἕνα σκυλὶ φοβισμένο ἀπ' τὴ σκιά του
γαυγίζει μόνο μὲς στὰ φῶτα τῆς λεωφόρου. Ὅσο ψηλὰ
κι ἂν σφεντονίσεις τὰ πράγματα, δὲ θὰ σταθοῦν στὸν ἀέρα,
δὲ θὰ βγάλουν φτερά· θὰ ξαναπέσουν μὲ γδοῦπο στὸ χῶμα,
στὸ ἴδιο σχεδὸν σημεῖο, σὰν τὰ νομίσματα τῆς τύχης,
δείχνοντας ἀκριβῶς τὴν ὄψη ἐκείνη ποὺ ἤθελες νὰ μὴ φανεῖ.

Ἀθήνα, 13.XI.72

THE EARTH'S ATTRACTION

A moon glued to the windowpane like a canceled postage stamp
on a letter undelivered. The closed furniture shop filled
with tables, armchairs, mirrors. A lone dog frightened by its
    own shadow
barks amid the avenue lights. No matter
how high you may sling objects, they will not remain in the air,
they will not sprout wings; they will fall with a thud on the earth
in almost the same place, like the coins of chance,
revealing exactly that side you did not want to appear.

Athens, 11/13/72

ΜΥΣΤΙΚΗ ΑΚΡΟΑΣΗ

Τὸ ἀπόγευμα εἴδαμε τὸ πλοῖο νὰ φεύγει ἀνάμεσα σὲ δυὸ κίτρινα
φύλλα.
Ὁ ἐργολάβος οἰκοδομῶν εἶταν πολὺ ὀργισμένος ἀπὸ μικρὲς
παραγγελίες.
Ἀργότερα ἄναψε ἡ ἀσετυλίνη τοῦ παντοπωλείου. Στὴν πόρτα του
κρεμόνταν
πλατιὰ κατάστεγνα φύλλα μπακαλιάρου. Ἀκουγόταν τὸ ἁλάτι νὰ
πέφτει
στὰ χαρτονένια κιβώτια. Ἐμεῖς δὲ μιλούσαμε διόλου μὴ καὶ
καταλάβει ὁ καταστηματάρχης
ὅτι γνωρίζουμε τὸν ἦχο αὐτό. Κείνη τὴν ὥρα ἐπιστρέφαν ἀπ᾽ τὸ
λιμάνι κάτω,
ἀπ᾽ τὰ σκαλιὰ τοῦ ναυτικοῦ ἐστιατορίου, ἀπ᾽ τὰ κλειστὰ ἰχθυοπωλεῖα,
οἱ τρεῖς τυφλοὶ μουσικοί. Ὅταν πλησίαζαν σ᾽ αὐτὸ τὸ σημεῖο
ἔκαναν τοὺς ἀκόμη πιὸ τυφλούς. Σταματοῦσαν στὸ πεζοδρόμιο
ἀντίκρυ
καὶ κούμπωναν ἀκόμη μιὰ φορὰ μὲ προσποιητὰ ἀμήχανα χέρια
τὴν πάνινη θήκη τῆς κιθάρας σὰ νἄντυναν μιὰ πεθαμένη. Δυὸ
κουμπιὰ
τῆς ραβδωτῆς γκριζόμαυρης ρόμπας της ἔλειπαν ἀκριβῶς στὴ θέση
τοῦ αἰδοίου.

Ἀθήνα, 14.ΧΙ.72

SECRET AUDIENCE

In the afternoon we saw the boat leaving between two yellow
   leaves.
The building contractor was greatly enraged to receive such small
   orders.
Later the acetylene lamp in the grocery store was turned on. By
   the door
hung broad dehydrated pieces of codfish. The salt could be heard
   falling
on the cardboard boxes. We didn't speak at all for fear the shop-
   keeper would understand
we had recognized the sound. At this moment, from the harbor
   below,
from the steps of the sailor's restaurants, from the closed fish
   shops,
the three blind musicians were returning. As they approached this
   spot,
they pretended to be blinder still. They'd stop on the sidewalk
   opposite,
and with hypocritically awkward movements of their hands
   would button up
the cloth case of the guitar once more, as though dressing a dead
   woman. Two buttons
of her striped gray-black dressing gown were missing, exactly on
   her vagina.

Athens, 11/14/72

211

ΔΙΑΡΚΗΣ ΟΦΕΙΛΗ

Νὰ χρωστᾶς πάλι. Νὰ θυμᾶσαι πὼς ξέχασες πάλι.
Νὰ π ρ έ π ε ι πάλι. "Ε, λοιπόν,—εἶπε. Σταμάτησε. Φαινόταν:
δὲν εἶχε τίποτ' ἄλλο νὰ προσθέσει. Λυπηθεῖτε με,—εἶπε—
κι ἅπλωσε ἀδέξια τὸν δείχτη του ψάχνοντας κάτι ἀκόμη νὰ δείξει.
Δὲ βρῆκε τίποτα ἐνθαρρυντικό, τίποτα βέβαιο. Κι ἄξαφνα
ἔδειξε ἐσένα· ὥσπου κ' οἱ τρεῖς μας δώσαμε τὰ χέρια
γύρω ἀπ' αὐτὸ τὸ λουλούδι ποὺ δὲν ξέραμε ἀπὸ ποῦ εἶχε ριχτεῖ.

'Αθήνα, 15.XI.72

CONSTANT DEBT

To owe again. To remember that he'd forgotten again.
That he *must* once more. Well then — he said. He stopped. It
    was obvious:
he had nothing more to add. Pity me — he said —
and spread out his net awkwardly, searching for something more
    to show.
He didn't find anything encouraging, nothing that was certain.
    And suddenly
he pointed at you; until the three of us joined hands
around this flower which had been cast down from God knows
    where.

Athens, 11/15/72

ΒΡΑΔΙΝΟ ΜΠΑΡ

Καρέκλες, ποτήρια, λαδωμένα χαρτιὰ ἀπὸ τυρόπιττες,
μεγάφωνα, λασπωμένα παπούτσια χτυπώντας τὸ ρυθμό, μάτια
θρησκευτικά, αἱματόστικτα, ψάχνοντας τὄνα τ' ἄλλο, ψιχάλα,
ὄγκοι καπνοῦ. Λίγο πρὶν εἶχαν φύγει οἱ πέντε ναῦτες
γιὰ τὰ σπίτια μὲ τοὺς κόκκινους γλόμπους. Στὸ βρεγμένο τζάκι
μιὰ ὑπόνοια ἐρωτική. "Ἂν λείψει κι αὐτὴ—εἶπε ὁ Θανάσης—
δὲ σώζεται ὁ ἄνθρωπος, δὲ σώζεται τὸ ποίημα. Ποιὸ ποίημα;—
ρώτησε ὁ Ἴων, ὁ πιὸ μικρὸς τῆς παρέας. Ἀπέναντι
σ' ἕνα τραπέζι μὲ πολλὰ ποτήρια, μόνος, ὁ νεαρὸς ἱπποκόμος
σχεδίαζε σὲ μιὰ χαρτοπετσέτα μὲ κόκκινο μολύβι
μιὰ ὁλόκληρη σειρὰ σταυρούς. Ἐμεῖς κοιτάξαμε πάλι τὰ τζάμια.
Ὕστερα φύγαμε. Τ' ἀδιάβροχά μας τὰ φορέσαμε στὸ δρόμο.

Ἀθήνα, 16.ΧΙ.72

EVENING BAR

Chair, water glasses, sheets oily with cheeseburgers,
loudspeakers, muddy shoes beating out the rhythm, eyes
religious and bloodshot searching out first one thing then another,
   a slight drizzle,
volumes of smoke. A little before the five sailors had left
for the houses with their red lights. On the wet windowpane,
an erotic hint. If this too were missing — said Thanásis —
man can't be saved, the poem can't be saved. What poem? —
asked John, the youngest of the group. Opposite,
on a table with many glasses, alone, the young stable boy
was sketching with a red pencil a whole row of crosses
on a paper napkin. We knocked on the windowpane again.
Afterward we left. We put on our overcoats as we walked.

Athens, 11/16/72

ΕΚΕΙ

Φωνές, λαχειοπῶλες, ἀνθοπῶλες, χαρτοπαῖχτες, θάνατος.
Ἄλλες φωνὲς ἀπ' τὸ σπίτι, ἀπ' τὶς κουρτίνες, ἀπ' τὰ ἔπιπλα,
ἀπ' τὰ λησμονημένα πορτραῖτα τῶν προγόνων. Ἡ γυναίκα σκυμμένη
κρατάει μὲ τὸ δεξί της χέρι τὸ φουστάνι της στὰ γόνατά της
σὰ νὰ φοβᾶται μὴ τῆς τὸ πάρει ὁ θόρυβος. Τὰ μαλλιά της
γέρνουν στὸ πλάϊ φυσημένα ἀπ' τὴν ἀνάμνηση. Κι ἄξαφνα
νιώθει τριγύρω στὸ λαιμό της, ἀβαρὲς σχεδόν, τὸ περιδέραιό της
σὲ μιὰν ἀνέγγιχτη στάση μελετημένης σιωπῆς—ἐκεῖ
ποὺ περιμένει πάντα ἡ ποίηση νὰ τὴν ἀνακαλύψουν.

Ἀθήνα, 17.ΧΙ.72

216

THERE

Shouts, lottery vendors, florists, card-players, death.
Other shouts from the house, from the curtains, from the furniture,
from the forefathers' forgotten portraits. The woman stooped
and with her right hand held her dress at her knees
as though fearing the noise might sweep it away. Her hair
leans to one side, blown there by remembrance. And suddenly
around her neck she feels her necklace, almost weightless,
in an intangible position of studied silence — there
where poetry always waits to be discovered.

Athens, 11/17/72

ΧΩΡΙΣ ΦΩΣ

Βράδιαζε μὲ μιὰ ξένη θλίψη. Αὐτὸς στεκόταν στὴν ἄκρη, ξεκομ-
μένος.
Δὲ φτάνει—εἶπε—ἡ φωνή. Χρειάζεται καὶ τὸ πρόσωπο πάντα,
χρειάζεται προπάντων τὸ σῶμα. Ἂν δὲν τοὺς βλέπεις
πῶς νὰ τοὺς ἀπαντήσεις; πῶς νὰ βρεῖς τὴ δική σου φωνὴ
καὶ τὸ ἀλάθευτο χέρι ποὺ ἀγγίζει, ποὺ πιάνει, ποὺ διώχνει; Στὸν
τοῖχο,
σ' ἐκείνη τὴν κλεισμένη ὀπή, τὸ ξέρω πῶς ἔχουν κρυμμένα
τὰ πέντε μεγάλα διαμάντια, τὸ ρολόϊ, τὸ γυάλινο μάτι, τὸ μέτρο
καὶ τ' ἄλλα τὰ πιὸ σιωπηλά, τὰ πιὸ πολύτιμα, ποὺ δὲν εἶταν κανεὶς
νὰ τὰ πάρει.
Σὰν κατεβαίνω τὴ σκάλα, μοῦ σβήνει τὸ κερί. Ἀπὸ κάπου φυσάει.

Ἀθήνα, 17.XI.72

218

LIGHTLESS

Night fell with an alien sadness. He was standing to one side,
    detached.
A voice — he said — is not enough. A face too is always required,
and above all a body is required. If you can't see them,
how can you answer them? How can you find your own voice
and the unerring hand that touches, that grasps, that chases away?
On the wall, in that closed hole, I know they've hidden
the five large diamonds, the watch, the glass eye, the tape measure,
and the other more silent, more precious things, when there was
    no one to take them.
As I was descending the stairs, my candle went out. There's a
    draft somewhere.

Athens, 11/17/72

ΑΛΛΑΓΗ ΒΗΜΑΤΟΣ

Δὲν εἶταν τίποτ' ἄλλο μὲς στὴ νύχτα ἐκτὸς ἀπὸ οὐρανός,
ἀπέραντος, ἀβέβαιος οὐρανός. Στὸ πεζοδρόμιο, στὴ γωνία,
ἕνα φανάρι φώτιζε τέσσερις πλάκες. Ὁ μικρὸς λοῦστρος
χτύπησε στὸ κασέλι τὴ βούρτσα του. «Ἄλλος», εἶπε. «Ἄλλος».
Κ' ἐγώ, ἄθελά μου, ἀκούγοντάς τον, ἄλλαξα πόδι σὰ νᾶταν
νὰ συντονίσω τὸ βῆμα μου μὲ τὸ νεκρό.

Ἀθήνα, 17.ΧΙ.72

CHANGE OF PACE

There was nothing else in the night but the sky,
an endless, uncertain sky. On the sidewalk, in the corner,
a lamp lit up four slabs. The young shoeblack
struck his box with his brush. "Next!" he said. "Next!"
And I, against my will, on hearing him, changed step as though
to synchronize my steps with the dead man's.

Athens, 11/17/72

ΑΘΩΩΣΗ

Ἡ παραλία ὣς πέρα εἶταν στρωμένη ψόφια ψάρια.
Τὸ πλοῖο ποὺ πλησίαζε εἶταν κόκκινο μὲ μιὰν ἄσπρη γραμμή.
Κάτω ἀπ' τὴ βάρκα, βγαλμένη στὴ στεριά, ἀναποδογυρισμένη
κοιμόντουσαν ἀκόμη μέσα στὴ λιακάδα οἱ δυὸ διαρρῆκτες
μαζὶ ὁ παιδεραστής, ὁ μουγγὸς κι ὁ νεκρόφιλος. Παράξενο—εἶπε—
νὰ ξέρεις ἄξαφνα πῶς δὲν ἔχει φταίξει κανείς.

Ἀθήνα, 17.XI.72

EXONERATED

The seashore all down its length was strewn with dried fish.
The approaching ship was painted red with a white stripe.
Under the overturned boat drawn up on shore, still
sleeping in the sunlight, were two burglars
together with a pederast, a mute, a necrophile. How strange — he
  said —
to realize suddenly that no one is to blame.

Athens, 11/17/72

223

ΣΥΝΕΧΕΙΑ

«Ποῦ πᾶς—εἶπε—μὲ τὴν ψεύτικη γενειάδα σου, μὲ τὸ ραβδί σου;».
    Ὁ ἄλλος:
«Βραδιάζει—ἀποκρίθηκε—ὅταν κανένας δὲν τὸ περιμένει».
Ἀπ' τὴν ἀπέναντι πλατεία εἶχαν φύγει κ' οἱ ἑφτὰ μπογιατζῆδες.
Μιὰ μακριὰ ταβανόβουρτσα εἶχε μείνει καταγῆς. Πόσα καὶ πόσα
κομμένα δάχτυλα—εἶπε—κρυμμένα μὲς στὶς λέξεις· τὰ βάζεις
πλάϊ - πλάϊ τόνα στ' ἄλλο· δὲ φτιάχνεις ἕνα χέρι. Τῇ νύχτα,
τὴν ὥρα ποὺ βγάζεις τῇ δεύτερη κάλτσα σου, ἄκρη - ἄκρη στὸ
    κρεββάτι,
βλέπεις τὸ χέρι τοῦ νεκροῦ νὰ παίρνει πάνω ἀπ' τὴν καρέκλα
τῇ γυάλινη κανάτα ὅπου ἔχεις ρίξει τὶς μασέλες σου καὶ τὰ κλειδιὰ
    σου.

                                                    Κάλαμος, 18.XI.72

CONTINUITY

"Where are you going?" — he said — "with your false beard and
    your cane?" The other:
"It gets dark" — he said — "when one least expects it."
All seven house-painters had gone from the town square opposite.
A long ceiling-brush remained on the ground. How very many
severed fingers — he said — are hidden in words; you place them
one next to the other, side by side; you cannot shape a hand. At
    night,
at the moment you're taking off your second stocking, on the far
    edge of your bed,
you see the hand of the dead man taking from the chair
the glass pitcher in which you've dropped your dentures, and
    your keys.

Kálamos, 11/18/72

225

Ἀπὸ πόρτα σὲ πόρτα τὸ βράδι μὲ γδαρμένους τοίχους.
Μιὰ μεγάλη σκισμένη κουρτίνα στὸ μπαλκόνι.
Ἡ νύχτα μὲ τὰ βήματα τῶν νοσοκόμων στοὺς διαδρόμους.
Μιὰ γραμμὴ μαῦρο αἷμα στὸ συσπασμένο στόμα
κ' ἡ γυναικεία κραυγὴ πλάϊ στὸ μεγάλο ρολόϊ:
«μόλις ποὺ πρόφτασαν καὶ τοῦδεσαν τὰ χέρια, θέ μου»,
ἐνῶ μπροστὰ στὸ παράθυρο περνοῦσε σκιῶδες τὸ πλοῖο
μὲ τὶς τρεῖς πεπλοφόρες. Τότε ἀκριβῶς ἀκούστηκε
νὰ πέφτει ἡ ἔνεση κάτω στὶς πλάκες. Ὁ ἀρχίατρος
ἔτρεξε νὰ σκεπάσει τὸν καθρέφτη τῆς εἰσόδου
μὲ τὸ σεντόνι τοῦ ἀρρώστου γιὰ νὰ μὴ δοῦμε ἀπὸ πίσω.
Ὕστερα τὸ πρωϊνὸ σπαρμένο μὲ σκισμένα χαρτιά.

Κάλαμος, 19.ΧΙ.72

TWELVE HOUR PERIOD

From door to door, the night with scratched walls.
A large torn curtain on the balcony.
The night, with the steps of orderlies in hospital corridors.
A line of black blood on the twitching mouth,
and a woman's cry beside the big clock:
"They've just barely managed to tie his hands, my God,"
while before the window a shadowy ship was passing
with three veiled women. At that moment exactly
the syringe was heard falling on the tiles. The head doctor
ran with the sick man's bedsheet to cover up
the mirror at the entrance that we might not see behind it.
Afterward, the morning strewn with torn papers.

Kálamos, 11/19/72

ΣΤΗ ΜΙΚΡΗ ΟΘΟΝΗ

Πάνω στὸ κεφαλόσκαλο εἶχαν μείνει δυὸ ρακέτες τένις.
Ἡ γυναίκα πρόφτασε κ' εἶδε μὲς στὸν καθρέφτη
τὸ χέρι ποὺ ἄνοιγε μιὰ φιάλη σόδας, κ' ὕστερα τ' ἄλογα
νὰ τρέχουν στὸ ρηχὸ ποτάμι,—ἡ ἴδια γυναίκα
ποὖχε ξεχάσει τὰ γάντια της στὸ ξένο σπίτι, πάνω
στὸν πορφυρὸ καναπέ, τὴν ὥρα ποὺ ἔξω στὸν κῆπο
φωνάζαν οἱ ἐπισκέπτες «τί μεγάλο φεγγάρι»,
«βγεῖτε νὰ δεῖτε τὸ φεγγάρι». Κι ὁ Πέτρος
στὴ δεύτερη αἴθουσα, μονάχος μὲ τὴν πεθαμένη,
ἔδιωχνε κάθε τόσο μὲ τ' ἀριστερό του χέρι
μιὰ μύγα ποὺ καθόταν στὸ στόμα της, γνωρίζοντας
μὲ μιὰ θλίψη ἰδιαίτερη ὅτι καθόλου μὰ καθόλου
ἡ ἐπιμονὴ τῆς μύγας δὲν ἐνοχλοῦσε τὴ νεκρή.

Κάλαμος, 19.XI.72

ON THE TELEVISION SCREEN

Two tennis rackets had been left on the stair landing.
The woman was in time to see in the mirror
a hand opening a bottle of soda water, and afterward
horses running in the shallow river — that same woman
who had forgotten her gloves in the stranger's house,
on its crimson couch the moment when in the garden outside
the visitors were shouting, "What a large moon!
Come out to see the moon!" And Pétros,
in the second drawing room, alone with the dead woman,
ever so often with his left hand chased away
a fly that kept settling on her mouth, yet knowing
with a personal sadness that the fly's persistence
was not annoying the dead woman, not at all.

                                        Kálamos, 11/19/72

229

ΤΟ ΑΓΑΛΜΑ ΤΟΥ ΚΑΦΕΝΕΙΟΥ

Αὐτὸ τὸ γύψινο ἄγαλμα κανεὶς δὲν ἤξερε πῶς βρέθηκε δῶ πάνω στὸ
   πατάρι
τοῦ λαϊκοῦ καφενείου,—πιθανὸν ἀπ' τὰ ἐκποιηθέντα φτωχοπράματα
κάποιου ἄγνωστου γλύπτη·—ἔτσι γυμνό, σκονισμένο, κλασικίζον
   κάπως,
ὡστόσο ὡραῖο μ' ἐκεῖνο τὸ ὕφος τῆς ἁπλῆς ἐφηβικῆς ντροπαλοσύνης
σὰ νἄθελε νὰ οὐρήσει κι ἀποσύρθηκε σὲ μιὰ γωνία, ἐδῶ ποὺ
   ξημεροβραδιάζονται
γέροι, ἀποτυχημένοι ἠθοποιοὶ μὲ βαμμένα μαλλιά, βαμμένα μάτια,
περιμένοντας πάντα μιὰ πρόσκληση. Κι ὅλοι ἔχουν δώσει σὲ γνωστοὺς
   καὶ φίλους
(ἂν κ' οἱ ἀποτυχημένοι καὶ φτωχοὶ δὲν ἔχουν φίλους) τὸν ἴδιο ἀριθμὸ
   τηλεφώνου, δηλαδὴ
τὸ τηλέφωνο αὐτοῦ τοῦ καφενείου. Κανεὶς ποτὲ δὲν τοὺς ζήτησε.
   Τώρα
σὰν κουδουνίζει τὸ τηλέφωνο δὲ στρέφουν πιὰ τὸ κεφάλι. Πίνουν
   ἀργὰ τὸν καφέ τους
σχεδιάζουν στὰ πακέτα τῶν τσιγάρων τους σπαθιά, στεφάνια δάφνης,
   τραγικὲς προσωπίδες
καί, κάποτε, νοερά, ἐρωτικὰ σχεδόν, πάνω σ' αὐτὸ τὸ γύψινο ἄγαλμα
   προβάρουν
λινοὺς χιτῶνες ρόλων ποὺ δὲν ἔπαιξαν, λησμονῶντας τὸ χρόνο,
πιστεύοντας πὼς τοῦτο τὸ ἄγαλμα εἰκονίζει αὐτοὺς τοὺς ἴδιους στὴ
   σωστή τους ἡλικία.

                                        Κάλαμος, Ἀθήνα, 19.ΧΙ.72

THE STATUE IN THE CAFE

No one knows how this naked statue came to be found on the
    mezzanine floor
of the popular cafe — probably from the auctioned wretched
    remains
of some unknown sculptor; thus naked, covered with dust,
    somewhat classical in style,
yet beautiful for all that, with the air of an adolescent's simple
    shyness,
as though it wanted to urinate and then withdraw into that corner
    where old men,
failed actors with dyed hair and painted eyes, spent their days and
    nights
waiting for a call forever. All have given to their friends and
    acquaintances
(even though the failed and poor do not have friends) the same
    telephone number, that is to say,
the number of this café. No one has ever called them. Now
when the telephone rings, they no longer turn their heads. Slowly
    they sip their coffee,
sketching, on their cigarette boxes, swords, laurel wreaths, tragic
    masks,
and at times, meditatively, almost erotically, trying out on this
    plaster statue
the linen tunics of roles they've never played, forgetting time
    thus,
believing this statue depicts their true selves in their true age.

                Kálamos, Athens, 11/19-20/72

ΑΝΤΙΔΙΚΙΑ

Κεῖνο τὸ πρόσωπο, πίσω ἀπ᾽ τὸ τζάμι, χωρὶς καμμιὰ σύσπαση,
παρ᾽ ὅτι κοίταζε μέσα στὸ ξένο σπίτι, μιὰ ἥσυχη νύχτα,—
θυμᾶμαι οἱ ἄλλοι δὲν τόχαν προσέξει. Ἔνιωσα μόνος
σὰν ἕνα καπέλο ξεχασμένο στὸ παγκάκι τοῦ κήπου
ποὺ ἐντός του πάγωνε λίγο - λίγο θολωτὸς ὁ ἀγέρας, ἐνῶ
μιὰ μαύρη πεταλούδα εἶταν καρφιτσωμένη στὸ φεγγάρι.
Τόδα κι αὐτὸ πάνω στὸ τζάμι, τὴν ὥρα ποὺ ὁ Ἀλέκος
ἔλεγε μὲ ἀδικαιολόγητα ἔντονη φωνή: «καμμιὰ ἀλλαγή,
καμμιὰ ἀλλαγὴ χωρὶς αἷμα». Κατάλαβα τότε πῶς κ᾽ ἐκεῖνος
τόχε προσέξει καὶ γι᾽ αὐτὸ ἀντιδικοῦσε μαζί μου.

Ἀθήνα, 21.ΧΙ.72

OPPOSITION

That face behind the windowpane, without a single twitch,
although it was looking into the stranger's house one peaceful
   night —
I remember that the others had not noticed it. I felt alone,
as though on a garden bench a hat had been forgotten
in which the domed air was very slowly freezing while
a black butterfly had been pinned to the moon.
I saw it also on the windowpane at the moment when Alékos
was saying in an unjustifiably intense voice: "There's no change,
there's no change without bloodshed." I understood then that he too
had noticed it, and for this reason opposed me.

Athens, 11//21/72

233

ΠΡΩ·Ι·ΝΗ ΑΝΤΙΝΟΜΙΑ

Ξημέρωσε ἕνα ἥσυχο πρωϊνό, τόσο διάφανο σὰν ἕνα δάκρυ
σταματημένο στὸ πρόσωπο τῆς γυναίκας ποὺ κοιμόταν ἀκόμη.
Πάνω στὴν πολυθρόνα τὰ δυὸ χέρια τοῦ ἀργυραμοιβοῦ κομμένα.
Τὰ γνώρισα ἀμέσως παρ' ὅτι δὲ μοιάζαν τόνα μὲ τ' ἄλλο—
τόνα ἀπ' τὸ σιδερένιο δαχτυλίδι, τ' ἄλλο ἀπ' τὴ χτεσινὴ γραντζουνιά.
Κι ἀντίκρυ, στὸ παράθυρο, πίσω ἀπ' τὰ λίγα φύλλα τοῦ δέντρου,
ἔλαμψε φευγαλέος, ὁλόχρυσος, ὁ γυμνὸς ὦμος τοῦ φονιᾶ.

'Αθήνα, 22.XI.72

234

MORNING ANTINOMY

A tranquil morning dawned, as translucent as a tear
halted on the face of a woman still sleeping.
On the armchair, the two severed hands of the money-changer.
I recognized them immediately—even though they did not
    resemble each other—
one by its iron ring, the other by a scratch made yesterday.
And opposite, on the window, behind the tree's few leaves,
gleamed, fleeting and golden, the naked shoulder of the murderer.

Athens, 11/22/72

235

ΤΟ ΙΔΙΟ ΘΕΜΑ

Δὲν ξέρω—λέει—γιατὶ φωνάζουν οἱ ἄνθρωποι
μιὰ καὶ τὸ ξέρουν πὼς κανεὶς δὲν ἀκούει. Ἐγὼ
κοιτάω ψηλὰ τὸ σύννεφο,—γέρνει τὸν ὦμο του.
Δὲν τὸ λέω σὲ κανένανε. Καθόλου δὲ μιλάω.
Ἴσως ἐλπίζω ν' ἀκουστῶ καλύτερα ἔτσι. Τὸ βράδι
εἶδα τὸ πλοῖο μὲ ἀναμμένα φῶτα νὰ περνάει
πίσω ἀπ' τὸ περιστύλιο. Κι ἄξαφνα
διέκρινα στὸ μάρμαρο τοῦ τραπεζιοῦ, νοθεμένη
τὴ σκιὰ τοῦ χεριοῦ μου. Τὴ σκέπασα ἀμέσως
μὲ τὸ ἴδιο μου τὸ χέρι, ἐνῶ ὁ παπλωματὰς
μὲ τὸ μακρὺ δοξάρι του ἔμπαινε στὸ τραῖνο
κάνοντας τάχα πὼς δὲ μ' εἶχε δεῖ.

Ἀθήνα, 23.XI.72

THE SAME THEME

I don't know—he says—why people shout,
since they know that no one is listening. I
look high up at the cloud—it tilts its shoulder.
I don't tell anyone. I don't speak at all.
Perhaps I hope to be heard better this way. At night
I saw a blazing ship passing
behind the peristyle. And suddenly
on the marble tabletop I discerned the shadow
of my hand, altered. I covered it up immediately
with the same hand, while the quilt maker
with his long archer's bow entered the train,
pretending he had not seen me.

Athens, 11/23/72

237

Νύχτες μὲ πυροβολισμοὺς καὶ τοίχους. Ὕστερα ἡσυχία.
Σφουγγαρισμένο πάτωμα. Τὰ πόδια τῆς καρέκλας ἴσα.
Πίσω ἀπ' τὴν πόρτα, ἡ δεύτερη πόρτα κ' ἡ τρίτη· ἀνάμεσά τους
μονωτικὸ μπαμπάκι ἀπὸ κεῖνο ποὺ κλείνουν τὸ στόμα
τῶν πεινασμένων ἢ τῶν πεθαμένων. Οἱ ἥρωες—εἶπε—
ἔχουν ξασπρίσει, θέ μου, ἔχουν χοντρύνει καὶ κοντήνει.

Ἀθήνα, 25.XI.72

1972

Nights with guns firing and walls. Afterward, quiet.
Scrubbed floors. The chair legs, straight.
Behind the door, a second door and a third; between them
insulating cotton of the kind used to stuff the mouths
of the hungry or the dead. The heroes—he said—
have grown white, dear God, they've grown fat and small.

Athens, 11/25/72

239

ΚΑΤΑΤΜΗΣΗ

Οἱ στρατιῶτες εἶταν κουρασμένοι· κάθονταν στὶς πέτρες.
Ἡ γυναίκα κοιτοῦσε ἀπ' τὸ παράθυρο. Βράδιαζε.
Ὀνειρευτήκαμε—εἶπε—μιὰ νίκη, ἢ τουλάχιστον μιὰ ἧττα
μιὰ ὁλόκληρη ἧττα. Μήτε αὐτό. Τίποτα. Ἐκεῖνος
ποὔχωνε μὲς στὶς φλέβες του σπασμένα γυαλιά,—νά τον
ἐκεῖ, στὸ τραπέζι μὲ δυὸ ἐπίδεσμους στὰ χέρια,
μοιράζει τὸ ψωμὶ φροντίζοντας νὰ πέσει
στὸ μερτικό του τὸ μικρότερο κομμάτι. Ὕστερα
τυλίγει τὸ μαχαίρι στὸν ἕναν ἀπ' τοὺς δύο ἐπιδέσμους
μὲ μιὰ λεπτόλογη ἱερὴ προσοχή, φανερὰ περιμένοντας
νὰ τὸν ρωτήσουμε ἀκριβῶς γι' αὐτὸ χωρὶς νὰ ξέρει τί ν' ἀπαντήσει.

Κάλαμος, 26.XI.72

PORTIONING OUT

The soldiers were tired, sitting on stones.
The woman was gazing out the window. It was growing dark.
We dreamed—she said—of a victory, or at least of a defeat,
a thorough defeat. Not even that. Nothing. He
who used to cram his veins with broken glass—there he is,
over there by the table with two bandages on his hands,
portioning out the bread and seeing to it that
the smallest piece falls to his share. Afterward
he'll wrap up the knife in one of his two bandages
with scrupulous and sacred care, obviously waiting
for us to ask him about precisely this, and he not knowing how to
    answer.

Kálamos, 11/26/72

241

ΚΑΤΩ ΑΠ᾽ ΤΟ ΣΥΝΝΕΦΟ

Μεγάλο μαῦρο σύννεφο σὰ θάνατος, προχώρησε ἀπ᾽ τοὺς λόφους
ἴσα πάνω στὴ θάλασσα, σκιάζοντας τὸν ὁρίζοντα ὣς πέρα,
σκιάζοντας καὶ τὸ μικρὸ καράβι ποὔχαμε διαλέξει. Δὲν ἔμεινε πιὰ
παρὰ ἡ μικρὴ τυφλὴ μὲ τὸ καλάθι της μπροστὰ στὸ καφενεῖο
καὶ τὰ πολλὰ ἀποτσίγαρα πατημένα μὲς στ᾽ ἄδεια βαγόνια τῶν
    τραίνων.
Τότε ὁ πατέρας τῆς τυφλῆς, τυφλὸς κι αὐτός, πλησίασε τὴν
    κοντόσωμη γυναίκα,
τῆς σήκωσε τὸ πηγούνι. «Ἐγὼ—τῆς εἶπε—θὰ σοῦ τὸ δείξω». Κι
    ἀμέσως
ἔγινε πάλι ἐκείνη ἡ ἀθωότητα μέσα στὸ κρύο τοῦ Νοέμβρη
ποὺ ἕνας - ἕνας ἀνάβαν τὸ κερί τους κι ἀνεβαῖναν τὴ σκάλα.

                                              Ἀθήνα, 28.XI.72

242

UNDER THE CLOUD

A large black cloud advanced like death from the hills
straight above the sea, darkening everything to the far horizon,
even darkening the small boat we had selected. Nothing remained
before the coffee house but the young blind girl with her basket,
and many cigarette butts trodden in the empty train carriages.
Then the blind girl's father, blind also, approached the stout
    woman
and tilted her chin. I—he said—will show it to you. And
    immediately
that same innocency occurred again in the November cold
where one by one they lit their candles and climbed up the stairs.

Athens, 11/28/72

243

ΤΑ ΜΑΤΙΑ ΤΟΥ ΑΓΑΛΜΑΤΟΣ

Αὐτὸ ποὺ φτιάχνεις γίνεσαι—ἔλεγε. Καὶ τὸ ἀμετάβλητο;—εἶπε ὁ
ἄλλος.
Ὦ, δικαιολογίες τῶν νωθρῶν, τῶν πολὺ πεθαμένων,—εἶπε ἐκεῖνος
καὶ βγῆκε ἀπ' τὴν πόρτα. Δὲν τὸν ξανάδαμε. Ἴσως νὰ τὸν σκότωσαν.
Εἶταν
ἕνας ἄντρας μετρίου ἀναστήματος, καὶ ξάφνου πῶς ἔγινε
ἕνα πανύψηλο ἄγαλμα στημένο μὲς στὸ ἴδιο μας τὸ σπίτι
πάνω ἀπ' τὴ σκάλα, μέσα στὸν καθρέφτη. Μᾶς κοιτάζει
μὲ τὰ λευκὰ μεγάλα του μάτια. Δὲ μᾶς ἀφήνει μιὰν ὥρα
νὰ κοιμηθοῦμε ἢ νὰ πουδράρουμε κρυφὰ τὸ πρόσωπό μας
μ' ἐκείνη τὴ θαμβωτικὴ χρυσόσκονη. Τί μάτια τεράστια
λευκά, κατάλευκα, τυφλὰ (τυφλὰ τὰ λέμε)· γυρνᾶμε
ἀπ' τὴν ἄλλη μεριά, πρὸς τὸν τοῖχο, βυζαίνοντας σὰ βρέφη
τὸν ἀντίχειρα τοῦ δεξιοῦ χεριοῦ του τυλιγμένον μὲ μπαμπάκι.

Ἀθήνα, 11.I.73

THE EYES OF THE STATUES

That which you make you become—he used to say. And the
    unalterable—said the other.
Oh, you justify the indolent, the thoroughly dead—he said—
and went out the door. We did not see him again. Perhaps they
    killed him. He was
a man of medium height, and suddenly how did he become
a towering statue erected in our own house
above the staircase, in the mirror? It gazes at us
with its large white eyes. It doesn't permit us for a moment
to sleep or to powder our face secretly
with that dazzling golddust. What enormous eyes,
white, pure white, blind (we call them blind); we turn
our backs, facing the wall, sucking like babies
the thumb of its right hand wrapped in cotton.

Athens, 1/11/73

245

Τὰ ἀκόλουθα ποιήματα ἀποτελοῦν ἕνα κύκλο μὲ τὸ γενικὸ τίτλο Δώδεκα ποιήματα ἀφιερωμένα στὸν ᾿Αραγκόν: «Σιωπηλὸ ἐγκώμιο», «Παράφωνη συγχορδία», «Ἐξαίρεση χωρὶς σημασία», «Στὴν ἄκρη τοῦ λιμανιοῦ», «Κατεδαφισμένα καταφύγια», «Μουγγό», «Ὑποτροπή», «Τρωτότητα», «Αὐτόπτης μάρτυρας», «Νυχτερινὲς συλλήψεις», «Συνήθης αἰφνιδιασμός», «Πραγματικὰ χέρια».

The following poems comprise a group entitled *Twelve Poems Dedicated to Louis Aragon:* "Meaningless Exception," "Mute," "Demolished Shelter," "At the Harbor's Edge," "Relapse," "Vulnerability," "Eyewitness," "Night Arrests," "Real Hands," "Habitual Surprise," "The Dissonant Chord," "Silent Praise."

91 **"Outline of a Nightmare."** Toward the end of his adventures, Odysseus and his companions were stranded on an island for thirty days. He made his companions swear a solemn oath not to touch any of Apollo's sacred cows pastured on that island; but ravaged by hunger, the crew caught several cows when Odysseus was asleep and slaughtered and ate them in a feast that lasted six days. When they launched their ship again, Zeus sent a great storm, on Apollo's complaint, so that the ship foundered and all but Odysseus were drowned.

101 **"The District Thimarákis,** 1939." "Thimarákis" is the name of the district in Athens where Rítsos lives, on Crow Street. "1939" refers to the eve of the war with Albania at the beginning of World War II.

155 **"Wintry Sunshine."** Chauteaubriand and Dórou streets in Athens were red light districts.

225 **"Continuity."** In the square outside the City Hall in Athens, housepainters who are out of work gather to make themselves available.

Yánnis Rítsos

The youngest of four children, Yánnis Rítsos was born on 1 May 1909 in Monovasía, southern Peloponnesos, the son of a ruined landowner. He began to write poetry at the age of eight, and is today Greece's most popular and prolific poet. He has published sixty-six books of poetry (in addition to some twenty selections as yet unpublished), two plays, a book of essays, and ten books of translations from French, Russian, Rumanian, Hungarian, Cuban, Turkish, and Czechoslovakian poets. He has been nominated ten times for the Nobel Prize (by a group of French authors, the PEN Club of Sweden, and Karamanlís's New Democracy party), and has been honored with the highest awards of every major European nation:

First State Prize in Poetry, Greece, 1956

Membership in the Academy of Arts and Sciences, Meinz, West Germany, 1970

Great International Prize in Poetry of the Biennial Knokkele-Zoute, Belgium, 1972 (other recipients include Guiseppe Ungaretti, Saint-John Perse, Jorge Guillen, and Octavio Paz)

International Award Dimitrof, Sofia, 1974

Great French Award in Poetry "Alfred de Vigny," Paris, 1975

Honorary Doctorate Degree from the School of Philosophy, University of Thessaloniki, Greece, 1975

International Award in Poetry "Etna-Taormina," Catania, Sicily, 1976 (other recipients include Salvatore Quasimodo, Dylan Thomas, Jules Superville, Jorge Guillen, Anna Achmatova, Giuseppe Ungaretti, and Rafael Alberti)

Lenin Prize, Moscow, USSR, 1977

Membership in the Mallarmé Academy, Paris, 1977

Honorary degree of D. Litt., University of Birmingham, England, 1978

249

His poetry has been translated into forty-four languages, among which are Bulgarian, Chinese, Czech, Danish, Dutch, English, French, German, Hungarian, Italian, Polish, Rumanian, Russian, Slovak, Spanish, Swedish, and Ukrainian. Since 1970 more than a half-dozen books have been devoted to translations of his poetry into English alone, and, significantly, more are in preparation.

Recognition of his poetry in his own country lagged far behind Rítsos's international fame, just as personal success escaped him in the midst of professional acceptance. His family life was replete with tragedy. An older brother, Dhimítris, and a mother only forty-two years old died within three months of each other of tuberculosis when he was only twelve; five years later he was himself stricken with the disease, and his father was confined to a mental hospital in Daphní, near Athens. His sister, Loúla, was institutionalized in 1936, the result of recurring mental problems. In and out of sanatoriums from 1927 to 1938, Rítsos continued to work, however sporadically, as actor, dancer, and poet. Upon the outbreak of war in 1941, he joined EAM (the Greek Democratic left) and followed its guerilla arm (ELAS) as it retreated before the British to northern Greece. There, in 1945, he participated in the Popular Theatre of Macedonia, which presented works extolling the actions of the partisans. Interned in a number of prison camps (Kontópouli, Makrónisos, Ághios Efstrátios) from 1948 to 1952, he thereafter enjoyed a fifteen-year period of respite — a prolific period during which he produced half his poetic output to date. The Papadhópoulos coup, on 21 April 1967, led once again to arrests, imprisonment, and exile on various Greek islands (Yéros, Léros, and Sámos) for almost three years. He was treated during this period for traces of cancer.

Today Rítsos divides his time between his winter home in Athens and his summer home on the island of Sámos, where his wife, Yaroufaliá Yeoryiádou, an influential leftist herself, practices medicine. His daughter, Éri, twenty-three years old, is a student in Paris. A confirmed "workaholic" (a habit he developed in confinement as a means of preserving both his art and his sanity), he spends every possible moment writing or painting. Well-received in a number of European art shows, he sketches on stones, bone, bits of wood and glass, making use of varied materials. Having survived the oppression of a tortured personal life, he has now to survive the rewards and expectations of an obsessive creativity.

Mr. Myrsiades first translated these poems literally, indicating in many instances the possibilities in the use of synonyms. Mr. Friar then polished the poems into their final form and checked the translations in many consultations with the poet. When a reader or critic is faced with a bilingual text, he is impelled to seek for a literal transcription in the translation. Although the translators of these poems have tried to keep as faithfully as possible to the Greek texts, their first consideration has always been to create good English poems. When a reader or critic may prefer one specific word to another as being closer to the original, he must keep in mind the translators' concern to choose individual words that also meet the over-all need of rhythm, orchestration, tone, and other aesthetic and technical considerations. A poem is not to be read in detail only but also as an entity in which the whole does indeed become much more than its parts.

Scripture of the Blind, by Yánnis Rítsos, was begun and completed in Athens in its first and second drafts between 28 September 1972 and 1 January 1973. The third draft was completed in 1973 during June and July in Athens, and during August in Sámos.